Cents & Sensibility

Cents & Sensibility

✦

The Practical Guide to Money & Aging

Martin S. Finn
John H. Lavelle

iUniverse, Inc.
New York Lincoln Shanghai

Cents & Sensibility
The Practical Guide to Money & Aging

Copyright © 2006 by Lavelle & Finn, LLP

iUniverse books may be ordered through booksellers or by contacting:

iUniverse
2021 Pine Lake Road, Suite 100
Lincoln, NE 68512
www.iuniverse.com
1-800-Authors (1-800-288-4677)

ISBN-13: 978-0-595-39481-4 (pbk)
ISBN-13: 978-0-595-83878-3 (ebk)
ISBN-10: 0-595-39481-7 (pbk)
ISBN-10: 0-595-83878-2 (ebk)

Printed in the United States of America

This book is dedicated to Ann & Patty for their unwavering support, dedication to family and the ability to tell us where to go when we need to hear it; and

To the Staff at Lavelle & Finn, LLP, who are constant reminders of what lucky men we are to have a second family at work, and who *also* tell us where to go when we need to hear it.

Contents

CHAPTER 6   Long-Term Care 56

Hope For The Best But Plan For The Worst

CHAPTER 7   Indispensable Insurance. 69

Cover Your Health and Your Life

CHAPTER 8   Investment Planning 79

Silver Heads and Golden Needings

CHAPTER 9   Defer and Conquer 93

How to Handle Your IRA After You Retire

Introduction

Life's certainties, it has been said, include death and taxes. To that list, in 21st Century America, two more can be added: an aging population and the resulting financial concerns.

In the year 2000, according to the U.S. Census Bureau, there were 35 million Americans age 65 and older. By 2030, demographers expect that number to more than double, to over 72 million. In that not-far-off year, one out of every five Americans will be a "senior," as traditionally defined.

During this period, the number of Americans 85 and older will double to almost 10 million. Centenarians, once a rarity, are now the fastest-growing segment of our population.

As seniors proliferate, so will their financial concerns. Even though some people keep working into their 60s, 70s and beyond, most people are no longer drawing paychecks at that stage of life. Employer-provided pensions are becoming rare while Social Security benefits generally deliver a small fraction of peak-career income.

Therefore, many seniors are concerned about running short of money during an extended retirement. Medical expenses, including long-term care, are an increasing burden among the elderly. In short, seniors are likely to feel a financial squeeze that will only tighten as they grow older.

This squeeze will affect not only seniors but their sons, daughters, and other loved ones as well. On one level, if seniors are forced to go through all of their assets to pay for living expenses, medical care, and long-term care, there will not be an inheritance to leave behind. Many middle-aged Americans now have expectations that the widely-publicized inter-generational transfer of wealth will make their own retirement more comfortable.

On another level, there is the possibility that impoverished seniors will call upon younger relatives for financial support. Caught in the middle between their aging parents and their own children, many middle-aged Americans may discover severe shortages of cash flow.

Considering the financial stresses on seniors and their younger loved ones, the bad news is not hard to find. Fortunately, there is a brighter side. Savvy use of family funds, skillful maneuvering through the tax system and knowledgeable application of government programs can help make retirement much more enjoyable for all concerned.

In this book, you will find an unsparing look at the problems faced by today's and tomorrow's seniors along with practical advice on how to solve them. If you are looking for get-rich quick investment advice, look somewhere else. The same is true if you are out to find slick tactics for evading taxes or tapping the government for undeserved assistance.

Instead, you will find proven strategies that seniors and their loved ones can implement to enhance the family's finances throughout a lengthy retirement, in sickness or in health. These techniques are sound, ethically as well as legally, and they are presented in clear, non-technical language.

Some of the topics addressed in the book include:

* **Investment planning**. Asset allocation is crucial for investment success and that is particularly true during retirement, when wealth accumulation may cease. In this case, it is critical to make the most of retirement assets already in hand.

* **Portfolio management**. Once it is time to tap an investment portfolio for spending money, hard decisions must be made. Is it better to take money from an IRA or from a taxable account? Sell stocks or sell bonds to raise needed cash? Sophisticated planning can lead to higher returns and lower taxes.

* **IRA distribution planning**. New IRS regulations make it easier to stretch out minimum required distributions and thus accumulate more wealth on a tax-deferred basis. Knowledge of those regulations is needed, though, so a thorough explanation will be provided.

* **Asset protection**. Seniors must be especially careful to preserve their principal because it will not be easy to recoup any losses incurred. This book includes extensive coverage of defensive measures, including insurance options and trust planning.

* **Housing needs**. Seniors may not be able to afford to maintain the house they have lived in for decades. Nevertheless, a desirable home is one key component of a happy retirement. Today, seniors have many options, from downsized condos to activity-rich retirement communities. Financing the right place may be difficult but possible for retirees who follow this book's suggestions.

* **Long-term care**. Perhaps the most vexing problem facing seniors today is the chance that they will require custodial care for long periods of time. High-quality nursing homes are not only expensive, but they present financial challenges now that the rules on Medicaid eligibility have been tightened. Fortunately, less costly and more appealing alternatives exist, such as home care and assisted living. Long-term care insurance may enable seniors to afford extended care without becoming impoverished.

* **Estate planning**. As has always been the case, this is a prime concern for retirees, who likely will want to provide for a surviving spouse and ultimately distribute assets among other loved ones. This book describes estate planning techniques for individuals and couples of moderate means as well as for those with significant net worth. Moreover, estate tax planning still is required because the future of tax legislation is uncertain. This book not only covers tax-reduction measures, it goes into astute uses of trusts such as providing for survivors with special needs.

So although death and taxes are a sad fact for all of us, it does not have to be all downhill once you retire. We feel certain that by reading on, you can make these effective techniques work for you on the road to your successful "happily ever after."

1

Basic Estate Planning

◆

Will-Power and Beyond

Many people think of "estate planning" as estate-tax planning. Such planning can be vital (see Chapter 4) but this perspective may lead you to believe that estate planning is only for the very wealthy. In truth, everyone should have an estate plan, no matter how munificent or how meager your net worth. Whether your estate winds up at $10,000 or $10 million, you are going to want to provide for your loved ones and your favorite causes. Putting together a solid estate plan not only will help you leave more wealth to your heirs, it will enable you to be certain that your wealth winds up in the right places as well.

What Goes Where

On the surface, estate planning may seem simple. First, you add up all of your assets, those you have now and those you expect to acquire in the future. Your assets might include cash in the bank, securities, retirement plans, real estate, insurance policies, and so forth. Subtract your debts and you have, in essence, your estate.

Next, decide where you would like those assets to go; to your surviving spouse, your children, perhaps your grandchildren. You probably have a religious organization or school or charity you would like to support, too. You might say 70% to your spouse and 10% to each of your two kids and 10% to your alma mater and that is your estate plan.

Generally, though, estate planning is not so simple. If you leave hundreds of thousands of dollars to your spouse, who never has handled large sums of money, will he or she be prepared to manage it well? If you leave a vacation home in Maine to your daughter who lives in Florida, will she be able to maintain the

1

property? One question, then, is whether your heirs are prepared to inherit. To address such concerns, communication is the key. You need to tell your heirs what you will be leaving them, and why. That will give them a chance to ask questions. Few people, however, make this kind of effort. A lot of parents are reluctant to give out information, even to their own children. Such reluctance, though, can lead to problems later on.

Help Wanted

In some families, logistics or personality clashes make it difficult to meet with heirs. If so, one technique that might work is to include a professional advisor in such meetings. That makes the meeting more businesslike and may help keep the heirs from being touchy about certain subjects.

Suppose, for example, you are working on your personal income tax return with your tax preparer. Many of your assets will show up on your tax return, in one way or another, so arranging a meeting with your tax preparer may be a good way to acquaint your heirs with what you have and how those assets perform. It is also a good way to acquaint them with your tax preparer, who may be able to help them after they inherit. Your heirs also should meet with your investment advisor, to learn what strategies you have been pursuing. If you own real estate, they should meet with the property manager. Of course, they should be familiar with the attorney who will be handling the estate's legal affairs.

Another good time for inheritance planning may be when you begin to take distributions from a retirement plan. You will probably name a beneficiary, usually a spouse or a child. You should include the beneficiary in your planning, explaining whether you are taking minimum distributions to extend tax deferral or whether you are taking out more money because you need the cash flow. This may help the beneficiary pick up the withdrawal schedule after your death.

Strategy Sessions

Some plans call for one beneficiary (a spouse) to roll over an inherited retirement plan and name a new beneficiary (a child), to defer income and increase the tax-free buildup. Such strategies should be understood by all the players when withdrawals begin.

Special situations may demand special attention. Jill Johnson, for example, has three children, including one who is disabled. Jill wants most of her estate to go to this child, meaning that the others will get less. Jill has explained this to the other heirs so that they understand; this is likely to avoid misunderstandings and hard feelings later on.

As a rule, should you divide your estate equally between your children, even if some are doing better financially than the others? That approach usually is most acceptable to all. However, you might want to leave more to a disabled child, as mentioned. In another situation, if you have given one child money to buy a house or start a business, the other children might get a larger share of your estate. In any case, this should all be explained to prevent dissension.

Blended families can be even trickier to deal with. If you have remarried and your second spouse is much younger, you will probably want to provide for her as well as for your children from your first marriage. In that situation, you might want a life insurance policy that will pay your children after your death, so they will not have to wait for years to inherit anything.

Basic Training

No matter what your family circumstances, there are some basics you need to have in place, so that your assets can pass smoothly to your survivors. Such items include:

A will. If you have been putting off making a will because you are too busy, too young, or not rich enough—or merely because the thought of your own demise is too much to bear—you should not delay any longer. Think of your family first, and prepare a will. Without a will, after your death a local court will appoint an administrator for your estate and your belongings will be distributed according to state law. Almost certainly, that disposition will not be exactly as you would like.

In some states, half of all your assets may go to your children if you die without a will. Minor children may become wards of the state, and your surviving spouse may have to account to a court for every penny spent on the children's behalf. Other relatives of yours, including your parents, may have no claim on your estate.

If you have a will, you have control: you can spell out the way you would like your assets to be distributed and you can name an executor, who will make sure your wishes are followed.

Once you have drafted your will, what should you do with it? You might keep it at home (telling loved ones where it is) or let your lawyer hold it. However, you should not leave your will in a safe deposit box. If you rent the box singly and you die, no one else will have access to the box.

If your will is held elsewhere, and the will names an executor, he or she can get a court's permission to open your safe deposit box. Just make sure that someone knows that you have a box, and where. You do not need to provide a key—a bank will drill open your box at a modest cost under a court order, providing access to the contents.

Letter of instruction. Although you should have a will, you cannot expect every item that you own to be covered in that document. Moreover, you should not change your will every time you buy a new car or change your investment strategy. Therefore, you should prepare a letter of instruction, sometimes called a letter of intent, to spell out exactly what your assets are and how you would like them distributed.

Suppose, for example, you have some valuable paintings you want to leave to your nephew or some jewelry you want a cousin to have. That type of bequest can be handled in a letter of instruction to the executor.

If you use a word processor you can update the letter from time to time, printing out a current copy. Of course, family members or unrelated parties should know where this letter is kept. Preparing such a letter may be a good way to avoid family fights over your favorite things.

Although your bequests should be discussed in detail with everyone concerned while you are alive, there may be some things you would rather not discuss during your lifetime. In that case, you might want to make a video recording, with a final message to your heirs as well as any instructions you care to provide. Even if you explain everything carefully to your heirs, it cannot hurt to go over it all again, on tape and in writing, so everyone knows exactly what you had in mind.

Some advisors recommend that everyone have a "death drawer," known to all the immediate family members. In that drawer you can leave a video and a letter of instruction spelling out your wishes for your property.

Other matters may be covered in this letter, from the identities of professional advisors to the location of key papers. In addition, you can use this letter to state your desires about funeral and burial arrangements. Some people have specified the music they want to be played, and the resulting service has been a powerful reminder of the decedent's personality.

Guardians. If you have minor children, your will should designate guardians, in case they become orphaned. Meetings and discussions with the potential candidates are essential before the final selection can be made. Use these meetings to find out about an individual or a married couple's willingness to become your children's guardian, their projected short- and long-range plans, and their viewpoints on issues that are crucial to you as parents.

Executor. As mentioned, in your will you can name an executor (sometimes known as an administrator or personal representative), who will "quarterback" your estate. After your death it will be up to your executor to inventory your assets, protect them against loss, pursue outstanding claims, pay bills, file tax returns, and pay taxes. (Even if there is no estate tax to worry about, there will be income tax returns to handle.) Your executor will be responsible for protecting your heirs and liable in case things go poorly.

A knowledgeable, conscientious family member who lives nearby may be a good choice. You probably should not name your spouse, though, because he or she probably will be too distraught after your death to act effectively. Often, grown children make the best executors. If that is not practical, you can name a professional advisor, such as an accountant or an attorney.

All executors will be entitled to statutory fees. However, family members may choose to waive those fees. On the other hand, your estate probably will have to pay professionals for their services so a fee schedule should be worked out in advance.

Whomever you choose to serve as executor, make sure you get his or her consent to serve before naming someone in your will. You should make some provision for a backup executor, in case your original selection becomes unable to serve. Then, go over everything with your executor. Your executor should know what your assets are, how the title is held, and where the paperwork can be found. Your executor should see your will, or at least know what is in it, so there will be no surprises.

If your executor is not a family member, he or she should meet your heirs, to get an idea of the personalities involved. Because your executor will be responsible for filing tax returns after your death, a meeting with your tax preparer likely will help things go more smoothly.

Trusts. Increasingly, trusts are not only for the super-rich. Many people of modest means create revocable trusts during their lifetime. Assets transferred into such a trust will avoid probate (see below). In addition, these assets can be managed by a successor, if you become unable to handle your affairs as you grow older. You also may want to create an irrevocable trust to hold assets after your death. That may be necessary if you think one of your heirs might squander the money or fall prey to con artists. A reliable friend, relative, or professional advisor can serve as trustee, who will manage the trust assets. A lifetime irrevocable trust is often used to reduce the value of your taxable estate and to protect assets from being eroded by long-term care costs.

Life insurance. If your income will be missed after your untimely death, you need some insurance. That is especially true if you have minor children. The trick is to buy enough coverage but no more. Determine what your family's income needs will be, what sources of income will be available, and how much life insurance will be necessary to provide the income that will be lacking.

Many financial advisors recommend that you have life insurance coverage of three to five times annual gross income. That is a rule of thumb that may vary, depending on your needs and financial circumstances. Your life insurance should be able to provide funds for:

- Any immediate needs your family may have at the time of death, such as medical expenses, funeral costs, estate taxes, or probate;

- Expenses your family may incur during a readjustment period, such as time for a surviving spouse to find a job;

- Income your family would need to maintain their standard of living;

- Your children's education and your spouse's retirement; and

- Paying off a mortgage or other personal and business debts.

Seniors might not need as much life insurance as people still in the work force, assuming that the seniors have grown children and substantial assets. Nevertheless, life insurance can provide a vital source of ready cash, so it should not be ignored.

To help you determine what kind of life insurance you should buy, you should consider the amount of coverage necessary to meet your obligations, the length of time you will need the coverage and affordability. Term life insurance will provide you with the maximum coverage for the lowest cost. Today, many parents choose 20 or 30-year term insurance, so they lock in a fixed price for the years when their children are dependents.

Your other choice, cash value or permanent insurance, provides an investment account in addition to pure insurance. For long holding periods, permanent insurance may be worth considering. The same is true for insurance you want to last throughout your lifetime.

Before buying any policy, it is advisable to look for a company that is licensed by your state insurance department and financially strong. A number of independent companies, including A.M. Best, Fitch, Moody's, Standard & Poor's, and Weiss Ratings analyze and rate the financial strength of insurance companies.

You can obtain such information from the insurer, your agent, public libraries, or over the Internet.

Funeral and burial arrangements. Does it make sense to pay for your funeral in advance? The main advantage of prepaying for funeral and burial arrangements is peace of mind. Your survivors will not have to make those arrangements during a time of stress. That is especially true if your loved ones live far away from you and travel delays might complicate matters.

Most funeral homes offer these plans. Ask your friends and acquaintances for the names of reputable funeral homes, then request their brochures. Buy the service you really want; do not let yourself get pressured into paying for unnecessary rituals.

Consult with your attorney before making any commitment and be sure to describe any arrangements you make in the letter of instruction that accompanies your will. Otherwise, your executor may pay again for funeral arrangements or a burial plot, unaware that you have already prepaid them.

Make sure your executor has all the details and any deeds or contracts are in an accessible place. Do not put your funeral and burial wishes in your will if the will is kept in a safe deposit box. The safe deposit box may not be opened until after the funeral—too late for burial instructions.

Technically, funeral arrangements are the responsibility of family members rather than your executor. However, there may be some confusion as to which family members should make the decisions. Because the executor eventually will pay the bills (out of your estate), it is probably better to entrust that person with the necessary documents.

Beneficiaries. Despite all the above comments about the importance of having a will, the truth is that the disposition of many assets will not be covered by your will. Retirement plans, for example, pass to designated beneficiaries regardless of what is in your will. The same is true of life insurance proceeds and certain savings or investment accounts that are "payable on death" to specified beneficiaries. Assets held in trust are not subject to the provisions of your will, either.

Therefore, it is crucial to keep beneficiary designations up-to-date so that they reflect your current wishes. The IRA you set up 20 years ago may still carry an ex-spouse as the beneficiary, for example; changing the designation now may save your family a lot of grief in the future.

Property ownership. There are essentially three ways to hold title to assets:

1. Fee simple. You own the property outright, by yourself. You can dispose of it as you wish.

2.   Tenancy in common. You own property with one or more co-owners. You may dispose of your share as you wish.

3.   Joint tenancy with right of survivorship. You own property with one or more co-owners. When you die, your share automatically passes to your co-owners.

Thus, jointly-owned property always passes to the surviving co-owner, no matter what you put in your will. If you change your brokerage account into joint name with your son Alan, at your death all of the securities in that account will go to Alan while your daughters Alice and Anne will be shut out. So you should consider changing from joint ownership arrangements, if that is not your intent, and be careful about adding one relative's name to your home, bank accounts, or investments.

If more than one sibling is involved, a trust may work best to protect all parties. The assets could be transferred into the trust and a specified son or daughter could be a co-trustee, empowered to act if you become incapacitated.

Despite the problems posed by joint ownership, seniors often see advantages in naming younger relatives as joint owners of their bank, brokerage, or mutual fund accounts. If you no longer can manage your financial affairs, a co-owner whom you have named can step in. At death, those assets will be transferred without going through probate (see below). This is an uncomplicated strategy that may work well without generating tax problems. However, certain joint ownership errors can have disastrous results so you need to be careful. Suppose you have $300,000 worth of securities with a $100,000 "cost basis" (the price you paid). If you die and leave your portfolio to your daughter Emily, current tax law permits her to inherit with a "step-up" in basis. That is, Emily will have a $300,000 basis in the inherited securities. She can sell them for $300,000 and owe no capital gains tax on the $200,000 worth of appreciation during your lifetime.

But what if you name Emily as joint owner during your lifetime so she can help you manage your portfolio? Will only half of this portfolio get a step-up at your death? Fortunately, the tax break need not be lost. If two co-owners are not married to each other, the estate of the first owner to die will include a share of the property based on the portion of the original purchase price furnished by the decedent. Thus, if you own securities outright and add your daughter as a joint owner, 100% of the securities will be included in your estate. Your daughter will get a full step-up in basis when she inherits.

The rules are a little different when it comes to real estate. If someone names anyone besides a spouse as a joint owner of real estate, including a personal residence, gift tax returns must be filed and gift tax may be owed. Nevertheless, the person whose name has been added to the property will inherit with a full step-up in basis at the original owner's death. No capital gains tax will be due on appreciation up to that point.

Joint tenancy can be unfortunate in the case of a second marriage, if each spouse has children from a previous marriage. When the first spouse dies, the survivor will inherit the jointly-held property, not the children of the spouse who died. Therefore, you might prefer fee simple or tenancy in common ownership, either of which gives you more adaptability.

Moreover, your situation will be different if you live in one of several states (including California and Texas) where community property laws apply. In essence, all property acquired by either spouse during a marriage as a result of the labors of either spouse is considered to be community property. Regardless of how such property might be titled, it belongs to a marital partnership between two 50-50 owners. Upon death, each spouse can control the disposition of his or her one-half community property interest. Thus, you only own half of community property, for purposes of deciding how to distribute such property at your death.

Negate Probate

The way that you hold property also can determine whether or not certain assets will have to go through probate, the process in which a local court supervises the distribution of your assets. In some states (California, for example), this process can be expensive and time-consuming. Nevertheless, there are steps you can take so that most of your assets will avoid probate.

Have a trust own your property. You can set up a trust and re-title assets so they are held by the trust. At your death, assets held in trust will not be subject to probate. In the trust documents, you can specify how the trust assets will be divided. They can remain in trust or be distributed to beneficiaries you name.

If probate avoidance is your main goal, a revocable trust is the usual choice. As the name suggests, a revocable trust can be canceled. If you change your mind, you can take back the assets into your own name. In most states, you can be the trustee and beneficiary of your revocable trust, so you can keep control of assets moved into the trust.

You should be aware that there will be costs involved in creating any type of trust. Assets must be transferred into the trust in order for them to avoid probate, so you need to go through with the paperwork. Moreover, certain assets, such as pensions and ownership of professional practices, cannot be transferred to a trust.

What about the tax aspects? Despite what you might hear or read, there are no tax advantages to creating a revocable trust. If you want to save income or estate tax, you must create an irrevocable trust, which permanently removes assets from your control.

Use joint ownership. As mentioned, a common way to title assets is "joint ownership with right of survivorship." If one co-owner dies, the others automatically inherit the property. Because of this automatic transfer of title, jointly-owned property does not go through probate. Thus, joint ownership is a simple, inexpensive way to avoid probate. In addition, a co-owner can handle the property if you become incompetent. On the downside, some sophisticated tax planning techniques may not be possible if too many assets are held jointly. You cannot leave assets to your daughter Barbara, for example, to take advantage of an estate tax exemption, if all of your property is held jointly with your spouse. Moreover, joint ownership robs you of flexibility, as explained above. At your death, everything in joint name will go to your co-owners, not to anyone else. It makes no difference what you put into your will.

Make maximum contributions to your retirement accounts. Put as much as you can each year into IRAs, 401(k)s, etc. For each account, make sure to name a beneficiary. At your death, the account will go to the beneficiary or beneficiaries you have named, without going through probate.

Besides probate avoidance, retirement accounts provide valuable tax deferral so you should use them fully. Money in these accounts may be protected from creditors, too. However, there are limits to the amount you can shelter in a retirement plan each year. In addition, you generally must start taking withdrawals from these plans after age 70-1/2. Once money is withdrawn, it is not sheltered from probate.

You should be aware that it is generally an error to name your estate as the beneficiary of your IRA or other retirement plan. If the money goes into your estate, it is subject to the time and expense of probate and your creditors. On the other hand, an IRA passing to a specified beneficiary skirts probate, as described above. So why should you put assets into your probate estate if you do not have to?

Invest where you can name beneficiaries. Most states offer payable-on-death (POD) and transfer-on-death (TOD) procedures for bank and brokerage accounts. A few even offer this option for motor vehicles. With these accounts, you name a beneficiary or beneficiaries to inherit the account after your death.

The accounts do not go through probate. Again, these designations are simple and inexpensive to put in place. They are flexible, too: you can change beneficiaries or close the account at any time. What's more, there are no limits on how much you can put in them.

The negative is the same as for joint ownership: the designated beneficiary gets the account at your death, no matter what it says in your will. Despite this similarity, you should not confuse a TOD or POD account with joint ownership. With the latter, each co-owner usually has full access to the assets and to any income it produces. With a TOD or POD account, the beneficiary cannot get at the account assets while you are alive.

Beyond POD and TOD accounts, life insurance policies and annuities also pass to beneficiaries you have named, without going through probate. Deferred annuities (fixed and variable), for example, permit you to defer tax on your earnings, perhaps for many years. Moreover, there are no required distributions: unlike IRAs, 401(k)s, etc., you do not have to start withdrawals from annuities after age 70-1/2, if you do not want to. Most annuities never require any distributions so the tax deferral may continue.

If an owner dies before annuitization, the annuity value is paid to the beneficiary directly without the delay and expense of probate. Moreover, annuities usually have an insurance feature that guarantees your heirs will receive either the amount you contributed plus interest or the market value of the funds in your account, whichever is greater. Some annuities have provisions that can deliver an even greater death benefit.

What if you die after annuitizing: that is, after converting your contract to a stream of payments? If you have chosen a "life" annuity, the asset dies with you. Guaranteed annuities, though, pay for a minimum period, no matter how long you live. Suppose, for example, Joan Brown buys an annuity and specifies a 10-year "period certain." If she lives for 25 years, she will get 25 years of annuity payments. However, if Joan dies after seven years, her beneficiary will receive payments for the remaining three years of the contract. Payments to Joan's beneficiary will not be subject to the delays and expenses of probate. Other types of payouts may be available. In any case, though, the monthly payment will be lower than the payment on a single-life annuity.

Although life insurance policies and annuities usually require you to pay sales commissions, they may be valuable if you want to be sure someone else has sufficient assets, after your death, or you want to save additional sums for retirement, on a tax-deferred basis.

You should save copies of all your beneficiary designation documents in case the financial institution loses them. Not only will this ease the transfer of assets, it can substantiate a claim that certain assets bypass probate.

Give away assets. Perhaps the simplest way to arrange for assets to avoid probate is to give them away while you are still alive. As of this writing, you can give away up to $12,000 worth of assets per recipient, each year, without worrying about gift taxes. If you are married, you and your spouse can give away $24,000 worth of assets, per recipient, per year. However, do not give away assets you think you might need eventually. Avoiding probate is a far less important goal than avoiding a cash shortfall.

Pave a Paper Trail

In addition to taking the steps described above, you should maintain a list of all your important documents, along with their location, to make life easier for your executor. Such a list also can:

- facilitate lifetime gifts, for estate-tax reduction;
- provide for an easier transition when the estate goes through probate; and
- help to determine the cost basis of securities, which will help the family resolve tax issues in the future.

Indeed, you should consider consolidating your securities. Many people have stocks literally all over the place, in their own name and at several brokerage firms. Those securities should be rounded up and held at one brokerage firm, making it easier for you and your family to keep track. If you want dividends and interest to be paid directly into a bank account, consolidation will make that easier to arrange.

Happy Outcomes

For a truly successful estate plan, you need to coordinate all of the various pieces—your will, your property ownership, your life insurance, your trusts—to get the results you want. However, there is more to a solid estate plan than a pile of paperwork. In addition to touching all the bases, you should sit down with your loved ones and explain how you have handled your assets, which advisors have been providing assistance, and what steps your heirs should take after they inherit. In fact, you should talk to all your close relatives while you are developing a plan, to avoid hard feelings in the family. Coming up with a plan takes some effort but your peace of mind will be worth it.

2

Incapacity Planning

◆

Worst-Case Scenarios

Naturally, your estate plan should focus on the disposition of your assets at your death. But what if you lose some of your cognitive abilities prior to your death and wind up making a series of bad decisions? Your estate could be a lot smaller than you had expected it to be, due to poor investments or the perils of falling prey to con artists. A sound estate plan should include some protection against incompetency. If you wait until you lose the ability to manage your own affairs, your assets may be jeopardized and a court will have to be petitioned to appoint a guardian. Such proceedings are expensive, time-consuming, and exposed to public scrutiny. In the aftermath, the appointed guardian may be required to post a sizable bond. Some steps you can take now, while you are still competent, will help you and your loved ones avoid such a painful process. You may, in fact, want to combine several of the tactics described below.

Joint Effort

The easy way to plan for incompetency is to put assets in joint name so either co-owner can act individually, if the other becomes incapacitated. Indeed, this might be the most common form of incapacity planning. When Aunt Mae fears that her health will fail, she adds niece Nora's name to her checking and brokerage accounts. If Aunt Mae cannot take care of her affairs, Nora can see that the electric bills get paid; stock dividends are deposited, etc. However, you might not want to hold all of your assets jointly. With joint ownership, the surviving owner inherits the property, no matter what you put into your will. If you have some other intent, joint ownership will not work.

Suppose you name a son or daughter as joint owner of any assets, including securities and real estate. No one else can inherit those assets. If you have other children, they will effectively be shut out. In addition to losing flexibility, you may incur gift tax consequences and lose the ability to do some estate tax planning, if all of your assets are held jointly. Moreover, if the younger person you name as co-owner has financial troubles, the jointly-held assets might be attached by creditors.

Personal factors should be considered, too. Some elderly people are comfortable, knowing that a friend or relative can write checks for them, but others are not. One practical solution is to keep small bank accounts in joint name, so there is ready access to cash in case of incapacity, while other assets are titled in some other manner. If you request direct deposits of income and automatic bill payments from checking accounts, such arrangements can reduce the need for joint titling.

Out of Joint

Joint ownership, moreover, will not solve all the problems that can be posed by incapacity. Take the example of Ida Davis, a widowed mother who lives hundreds of miles away from her children. Ida refuses to admit that she needs help, even though she has left candles burning and eaten spoiled food. Her children have hired a geriatric care manager to help out but Ida refused to cooperate.

In such circumstances, choices are painful. Ida's children might just leave her alone, running the risk she will harm herself or others. Alternatively, they might ask a court to name a guardian, but such proceedings often stir up hard feelings. The decision might be easier if there is agreement on how to proceed among family members, but such agreement may not be easy to reach.

To see a better solution, take the example of Henry Madison, who is beginning to show signs of mental deterioration. Fortunately, all clients of Henry's attorney fill out power of attorney forms, as a standard procedure. In this case, Henry's daughter Paula, who has the power to act for her father, is extremely competent. Thus, there is less risk that Henry will mismanage his affairs.

Power Plays

Indeed, professional incompetency planning usually begins with a power of attorney, a document that names an agent, also known as an "attorney in fact," who can sign checks, pay bills, file tax returns, make gifts, disclaim property, make retirement plan distribution decisions, etc., on behalf of you, the principal. (The power can name more than one agent, stating whether they may act singly or if they must act in concert.)

A run-of-the-mill power of attorney (the short form you can pick up for a few dollars at a stationery store) is *nondurable*, meaning that it will no longer be effective if you lose your capacity to make decisions. On the other hand, a *durable* power of attorney remains in effect even if you become incapacitated. Virtually every state recognizes a durable power of attorney.

Relying upon powers of attorney makes sense on paper but there may be real-life concerns. Many people are reluctant to sign a power of attorney and give someone else control over their assets. You need to trust your agent absolutely.

Unlike guardians, agents generally are not monitored by a court. Consequently, misuse of funds may go unnoticed. What's more, you should name at least two successor agents, if your first choice cannot serve, and those successors also must inspire your confidence.

As a safeguard, the document might state that the power will go into effect only if you are judged incompetent by a person named in the document, for example, your personal physician. Such contingent powers are called "springing" powers, also accepted in most states.

Can you rely upon a springing power? Some advisors prefer a full power of attorney, not a springing power. If someone becomes incapacitated, the situation is stressful enough. You do not want hassles with a bank or brokerage firm. That is, it may be difficult to establish someone's incompetency, especially in case of an on-again, off-again incapacity, so it may be difficult for a springing power to take effect.

For such reasons, some attorneys favor durable powers because they are more convenient. However, if you are not comfortable knowing that your agent can use the power of attorney at any time, to take over your assets, you might choose the springing power.

Powers That Be

Perhaps more important, you also should hire a knowledgeable lawyer to draw up your document. An oversight can be extremely costly.

In one case, for example, an elderly woman appointed her nephew as her agent on a durable power of attorney when she was extremely ill. (In fact, she died two months later). The nephew, wishing to reduce estate taxes, made 38 gifts of $10,000 apiece to various friends and relatives. Under the law in effect then, those gifts could be covered by an annual tax exclusion and removed from the aunt's estate, tax-free. The IRS attempted to restore this $380,000 to the aunt's estate, and the issue wound up in court. The nephew testified that he had discussed the idea of making gifts, in order to reduce estate taxes, with his aunt. According to the nephew, he drew up a list of 40 possible recipients, read the names to his aunt, and received 38 nods of approval from his weakening aunt.

This testimony did not convince the court. These events took place in California, where powers of attorney must specifically state that the agent has the authority to make gifts on the principal's behalf. (Many states have similar laws.) Here, the power of attorney did not include this authorization so the gifted assets were effectively returned to the aunt's taxable estate, at a cost of over $140,000 in estate tax. Therefore, if you choose to include a power of attorney in your estate plan, make sure that it spells out the agent's ability to make gifts, to family members or to non-relatives.

Besides this gifting power, other specific authorizations should be included in your power of attorney. Your agent should be permitted to create and fund trusts, for example, and replace trustees who prove to be unsatisfactory. In addition, your agent should be authorized to interface with Social Security, Medicare, and other government agencies.

You might not want to limit a power of attorney to your own assets. Many people, after accumulating sizable estates, put assets into their spouse's name, for wealth protection or estate tax reduction. In those cases, there is a danger that the spouse will become incapacitated, unable to manage those assets. Both spouses should be covered by powers of attorney.

Valid Objections

In practice, some financial institutions are very reluctant to accept powers of attorney unless their own forms are used. They are concerned about the liability they might have if they permit transactions under a form that is not valid. Therefore, you should send a copy of your power to every bank, broker, etc., with whom you do business, to see if there is any problem.

After you execute a power of attorney, you should update it every year or two, which will increase the likelihood your power will be honored. Some securities transfer agents and property title companies will not accept old powers for fear that a challenger with an adverse interest may claim that it is invalid. Each time your power is renewed, have at least original powers of attorney executed and notarized, because some institutions may insist upon keeping one of these powers in their files.

Turning to Trusts

Besides a durable power of attorney, you may need a revocable trust as part of an incapacity plan. Many promoters advertise the wonders of "living" or "loving" trusts. Indeed, such trusts offer many advantages to their creators. However, the claims advanced for these trusts are often misleading and sometimes outright wrong. If you know the real benefits and drawbacks you can construct a trust with the features that best meet your needs. To put revocable trusts in context, it helps to know some definitions. Trusts are sliced into two categories:

Living ("inter vivos") trusts are established while the creator is alive.

Testamentary trusts go into effect after the grantor's death, as spelled out in a will.

Then, living trusts are diced into two further types:

Revocable trusts can be materially changed or canceled altogether.

Irrevocable trusts cannot be rescinded after they go into effect. You generally will not have access to assets you have transferred to an irrevocable trust and you cannot maintain any control over the trust if you wish to reap the benefits an irrevocable trust can offer.

As you would suspect, a revocable trust must be a living trust. In practice, most mentions of "living" trusts really refer to revocable trusts. When you create a revocable trust, you generally can serve as trustee and beneficiary. Therefore, you can retain control over any assets you transfer into the trust. If your plans or marital status change, you can revoke the trust and take personal possession of those assets once more.

Successful Succession

As indicated, a revocable trust can prove to be valuable in case you become incapacitated. If you become ill or mentally incompetent, a successor trustee can take over management of the trust assets. There will be no costly, public, time-consuming court battle over control of your finances.

Here is how a revocable trust can work: When you create your trust and name yourself as trustee, you also select a successor trustee. You might designate co-successors, perhaps including an institution that will assume financial responsibility. Some banks and brokerage firms that balk at accepting powers of attorney willingly deal with successor trustees. When the trust is created you should spell out the circumstances in which you no longer can manage your own affairs, and who will make the determination. For example, two doctors might have to state in writing that you are incapacitated. If this should occur, the successor trustee can step in immediately. Moreover, the successor or successors will have a fiduciary responsibility to protect your interests.

Privacy, Please

With a living trust and a power of attorney, your loved ones can avoid seeking a conservatorship or guardianship, a process that is extremely cumbersome, costly, and frustrating. Within the privacy of a trust, the change of control over valuable assets may be much smoother.

Many seniors prefer the idea of a successor trustee to a co-trustee, so they can remain in control, as sole trustee. However, at some point, if they think they are slowing down, it may be time to add a son or daughter as co-trustee. Adding a co-trustee may be easier for people to accept, rather than resigning and letting a successor trustee take control of the trust assets.

Such a plan, of course, assumes that there are assets in the trust to control. With a living trust, you must transfer assets into the trust, in order to get the advantages. Some people do not follow through. Moreover, diligence is required, long after a trust is created, because new assets might be acquired and not titled properly. Therefore, seniors need to follow up after living trusts are created. Just about anything can go into the trust—tax-deferred retirement accounts, including IRAs, cannot be held in the trust, though.

Can that last exclusion cause problems? Indeed, a large IRA may disrupt the planning process and create some challenges. Therefore, it is usually better for seniors to automate their finances as much as possible, perhaps by arranging for automatic IRA distributions, when they are appropriate. Especially with seniors who rely heavily on a large IRA, which cannot be held in a living trust, it is important to have a power of attorney in place and to be sure the power will be recognized by the IRA custodian. If you become incompetent, your agent will have access to your IRA via the power of attorney.

Looking Out For Number One

To see how a revocable trust can work, consider the case of Lou Thomson, whose estate was to go to his two nieces. As he grew older, he no longer could care for himself. His nieces, then, could provide him with quality long-term care in an expensive nursing home. Or, they might neglect Lou, hoping to preserve the assets that they would eventually inherit. Fortunately, Lou had drawn up a revocable trust, naming a local bank along with the nieces as successor trustees. The trust documents called for the successors to provide the best care for Lou, if necessary, and the bank made sure this instruction was carried out, to Lou's comfort.

As another example of how a backup trustee can become the primary trustee without a public court battle or private family skirmishes, consider how a revocable trust served Rhonda King, who had a heart attack just before closing on a house sale. She was in intensive care but her son, the backup trustee, took over and sold the house, which was held in the trust. Without that trust, the deal might have fallen through.

Probate-Proof

Often, revocable trusts are promoted heavily as a means to circumvent the time and expense of "proving" a decedent's will to a local court. In most states, though, probate is not that burdensome or expensive. Many localities offer a simplified probate process that your heirs may be able to use. What's more, many types of assets are excluded from probate anyway, whether or not you have a revocable trust. They include jointly-held property, which passes to the surviving owner, as well as insurance proceeds and retirement accounts (including IRAs), which go to the designated beneficiary.

Probate may be a real hassle, though, if you own property in another state. Your survivors will have to go through a separate probate for the out-of-state asset. That may mean hiring an attorney, long-distance, or making unwanted trips. In such cases, a revocable trust may be worthwhile because holding out-of-state property in a revocable trust avoids this "ancillary" probate as well as local probate.

Yet another benefit of creating a revocable trust is the need to get your affairs in order. This will help you manage your affairs as you grow older and assist your heirs in handling your estate. For example, Carla Jones created a revocable trust and began the process of re-titling her assets to the Carla Jones Trust. She discovered she had 19 mutual funds, six brokerage accounts, and three bank accounts. In re-titling her assets she consolidated them into a few accounts so recordkeeping is easier while expenses have been reduced.

If those are the pros of revocable living trusts, what are the cons?

No tax benefits. Despite what you might hear or read, revocable trusts are tax-neutral. For income tax purposes, trust income is taxed to you, as the grantor. For estate tax purposes, assets transferred to a revocable trust are included in your taxable estate.

Misinformation about revocable trusts can lead you to neglect necessary tax planning, especially when it comes to estate tax. On the bright side, virtually all sophisticated estate and income tax planning strategies can be used in conjunction with revocable trusts.

No asset protection. Assets held in a revocable trust are just as vulnerable to your creditors as assets you hold personally. For example, if you hold rental property in a revocable trust, a tenant whose child eats led paint may sue you personally for damages. Other forms of ownership, such as a limited liability company (LLC), should be used.

Administrative hassle. After creating a revocable trust you must make the effort to re-title assets from individual ownership to the trust. Assets not formally held in the trust will have to go through probate and will not be under the management of a successor trustee, in case of incapacity.

Cost. Moreover, you will incur some legal fees when you create a revocable trust, fees that will vary by area and by the complexity of the documents. In most situations, however, the cost of creating a revocable trust will be greater than the expense of having a will drafted. Do not work with an attorney who advertises cheap living trusts. The key to the creation of such a trust is the transfer of assets into it; these trusts are not effective unless properly funded. Deciding which assets to transfer into the trust, properly handling beneficiary designations, and the certainty of legally valid transfers are as important as the creation of the document itself.

Complacency. Merely setting up a revocable trust will not provide you with a complete estate plan. You also should:

- Take the time to re-title assets to the trust.

- Have a will to cover those assets not held in the trust.

- Select suitable trustees, get their agreement to serve, and make arrangements for backup trustees.

- Work with a knowledgeable professional on tax planning.

- Explain all of these arrangements to your heirs.

His and Hers or Ours?

Married couples must decide whether to use a joint revocable trust or to have each spouse create his or her own trust. Often, individual trusts are the better choice. If the IRS imposes a lien against one spouse, the assets in the other spouse's trust might not be jeopardized. In addition, if one spouse dies, the survivor may have easier access to the assets in his or her own trust than would be the case with a joint trust.

Final Thoughts

In addition to a revocable trust and a power of attorney, other components should be included in an incompetency plan. You should also execute a health care power of attorney, (or proxy, in some states) for example. If you are unable to make medical decisions, someone else can. You can name a different agent for a health care power of attorney than for a durable power of attorney; for a health care power, you will want a compassionate person rather than someone with good business sense.

Hospitals and doctors are legally required to honor the decisions of your appointed agent. Not only should you carry a copy of this proxy with you at all times, copies also should be held by your agent, your primary physicians, and your local hospital. Language in this proxy should specifically authorize the release of your medical information to your appointed agent. Otherwise, federal law might limit such release, making it difficult for your agent to make informed decisions.

Similarly, you may want to draw up a living will. Living wills do not replace traditional wills but they state the circumstances in which someone will want doctors to withhold or withdraw life support systems. In addition, if you are not married you may want to draft a document granting visitation rights to certain loved ones in case you are hospitalized.

Personal Best

Incapacity planning is an ongoing process, one that must be refined as circumstances change. All of the documents discussed in this chapter need to be updated on a regular basis to take into account changing laws and different preferences for who should be named to act on your behalf.

3

Income Tax Planning

✦

The Tax Man Cometh

Retirees, by definition, have no earned income. Therefore, many people must tap their investment portfolios for spending money. Especially in these days of low yields on bonds and bank accounts, that is not easy to do. You need to be savvy when deciding how to invest, which investments to sell, and whether to draw down your IRA or your taxable accounts. In particular, you can boost your net income by reducing the taxes you incur. Here are some suggested tactics.

- If you start receiving Social Security benefits at the youngest possible age (62), avoid selling appreciated securities in taxable accounts. By not taking gains, you will hold down your adjusted gross income (AGI), which may lower the tax you will owe on your Social Security benefits (see below). In addition, if you do not sell appreciated securities, you may die still owning them. Your heirs might get a basis step-up, depending on tax law at that time. If so, no income tax will be paid on the appreciation of those investments during your lifetime.

- Similarly, if you start receiving Social Security at age 62 you should postpone taking IRA distributions until they are required, after you reach age 70-1/2. Such a delay can mean that:

  1. your IRA will continue compounding, tax-deferred;

  2. your AGI will not be increased by the receipt of IRA distributions, which can trim tax on your Social Security benefits; and

  3. a greater amount of your IRA will be left to your heirs.

- Take unrealized capital losses in taxable accounts. If you postpone tapping your IRA, you may need to raise money from your taxable accounts. Your first step should be to sell stocks and stock funds with unrealized capital losses. Up to $3,000 worth of net capital losses can be deducted against ordinary income each year while excess losses can be carried forward to future years. On the other hand, if you decide not to take losses and you die with such stocks or funds, the unrealized capital losses will not provide any tax benefit. What's more, at your death, a capital loss carryover will be extinguished. The sooner you sell stocks to realize losses, the better the chance that the capital loss carryover will be used before death, to offset any capital gains you realize. In addition, taking the loss may lower your AGI and reduce the tax you will owe on your Social Security benefits.

- Next, use up income-producing assets (bank accounts, for example) you will reduce the tax bills they generate and allow tax-advantaged assets to stay in place. Eventually, you can redeem any U.S. Savings Bonds you own, which will trigger all the deferred income tax. By waiting to redeem these bonds as long as possible, you will benefit from ongoing tax-deferred accumulation of interest. Also, waiting to redeem your Savings Bonds, increases the possibility that you will be completely retired with no earned income. Then the reported interest from your Savings Bonds may be taxed at a lower rate.

Do not take capital gains until after you cash in your Savings Bonds. As mentioned, an appreciated stock's basis may be stepped up at your death, saving income tax. In contrast, Savings Bonds generate income in respect of a decedent (IRD), so they will be taxed after your death. You might as well cash them before you take gains on appreciated stocks and stock funds.

- If you have substantial amounts of appreciated securities, withdraw money from your IRA before taking gains in your taxable account. As long as the appreciated assets (stocks and stock funds) in your taxable accounts produce low dividends, your annual tax burden will not be that great. However, if your taxable accounts hold tax-inefficient mutual funds that regularly generate capital gains distributions, you probably should liquidate such funds before tapping your IRA. Otherwise, hold your appreciated assets and withdraw from your IRA. At your death, your heirs may inherit highly-appreciated taxable securities and a smaller IRA. Again, your heirs may receive a basis step-up for the appreciated assets. They can continue to hold such investments in the taxable accounts without having to take taxable withdrawals. On the other hand, your heirs will be required to take withdrawals from an inherited IRA, there is no basis step-up, and the amounts they withdraw will be taxed as ordinary income. For these reasons, it is better to bequeath your heirs highly-appreciated stocks and funds, rather than a plumper IRA.

Social Insecurity

Your investment and financial planning also may be affected by the possibility of an income tax on your Social Security benefits. This tax involves a bizarre concoction known as "provisional income." To calculate provisional income, you add:

Adjusted gross income (AGI). You get this number from the bottom of the first side of your federal income tax return.

Tax-exempt interest income. As a result, tax-exempt income effectively becomes taxable income, in some situations. This includes interest from municipal bonds and municipal bond funds.

One-half of your Social Security benefits.

Suppose, for example, you and your spouse have AGI of $30,000. You receive $1,000 per year in tax-exempt interest and Social Security benefits of $1,200 per month. Thus, your provisional income would be $38,200:

AGI	$30,000	
Tax-Exempt Interest	1,000	
½ of Social Security Benefits	7,200	($1,200 x 12 = $14,400;
		$14,400/2 = $7,200)
Provisional Income	$38,200	

On a joint return, you can have provisional income up to $32,000 without having to pay any tax on your Social Security benefits (single filers can have up to $25,000 in provisional income.)

Here, your provisional income is over the limit by $6,200. The next step is to take half of that number ($3,100) and compare it with half the amount of Social Security Benefits ($7,200). The smaller amount ($3,100, in this example) is the amount that is added to your taxable income. The way the math works, up to 50% of your benefits can be taxed.

If your provisional income, as calculated above, is greater than $44,000 on a joint return or $34,000 filing singly, you have an entirely different set of calculations to contend with. Here is the outcome of those calculations:

Joint returns. With provisional income of $44,000, 50% of your Social Security benefits will be taxed. When your provisional income is above that level, the percentage to be taxed escalates rapidly. Once it reaches $50,000, 85% of your benefits will be taxed.

Single filers. At $34,000 in provisional income, 45% of your benefits will be taxed. (It seems like the percentage should be 50% but the math is a bit complicated.) Again, the percentage escalates with your provisional income, so that 85% of your benefits will be taxed when you reach $44,000 in provisional income.

Note that is not the same as saying that your benefits will be subject to a 50% or an 85% tax rate. If 85% of your benefits are taxed, and you are in a 33% tax bracket, about 28% of your Social Security benefits will go to the IRS.

Maneuvering In The Middle

The bottom line, then, is that if your provisional income, as defined, is below $32,000 on a joint return ($25,000 for single filers), your Social Security benefits will not be taxed. This entire subject is a non-issue.

On the other hand, if your provisional income is well over $50,000 on a joint return or $44,000, filing singly, there is not much you can do about it—85% of your Social Security benefits will be taxed.

In between, though, a little planning can have a large payoff. That is, if your provisional income is between $32,000 and $50,000 on a joint return (between $25,000 and $44,000, filing singly), you should take steps to shelter yourself from the tax. If you can lower your provisional income, you will enjoy more of your Social Security benefits.

(If you are married filing singly, and you have lived with your spouse at any time during the year, up to 85% of your Social Security benefits will be included in your taxable income, despite any tax planning.)

How can you reduce your provisional income and cut the tax on your Social Security benefits?

Rearrange your investment portfolio. The conventional wisdom holds that retirees should put their money largely into bonds (taxable or tax-exempt) to maximize retirement income. That is true, if you need the interest income for living expenses.

However, you are probably better off putting your money into stocks or stock funds. Over the years, you will likely get higher returns from stocks than from bonds. What's more, if you do not take profits from your stocks, you will generate little or no current income, so your Social Security benefits will not be taxed as heavily.

When you have to liquidate securities for living expenses, take losses. Any losers that you sell can offset capital gains you realize. As mentioned, up to $3,000 worth of net capital losses can be deducted each year, which will reduce your AGI and your provisional income.

Stagger your income. If you are withdrawing from your IRA or liquidating appreciated investments for retirement income, you have some control over your finances. For example, you can increase your sales and withdrawals late in the tax year, biting the tax bullet, and build up enough funds so you can minimize those activities in the following year, reducing your provisional income that year.

If you must tap your IRA for living expenses during retirement, you might take out two years' worth of living expenses this year. Next year, if you are not required to take withdrawals, you might be able to live off of the proceeds without taking money from your IRA. Every other year, then, your AGI and provisional income might fall, giving you a year off from highly-taxed Social Security benefits.

Use your borrowing power. If you need money, you can sell some stocks, but taking gains would trigger tax obligations. Instead, you can borrow against the stocks—the proceeds from margin loans are not counted as income, for income tax or for the tax on Social Security benefits. The same holds true for all types of loan proceeds. You can borrow against a home equity line or a life insurance policy; you can enter into a reverse mortgage secured by your personal residence. All of these strategies give you cash flow—spending money—in retirement without triggering tax obligations. You may even cut your income tax bill by paying deductible interest.

Defer taxable income. Another type of investment might be appropriate if you are in this income range ($25,000-$50,000) and you do not need all of your investment income to live on: a deferred annuity. Many insurance companies offer deferred annuities and so do other types of financial companies. The idea is that you put money into a deferred annuity and enjoy tax-free buildup until you take the money out.

Deferred annuities come in two varieties:

Fixed annuities. You can expect to receive the type of return you would receive from a high-quality corporate bond. Fixed annuities work like CDs—your account balance goes up but not down—with tax deferral providing another advantage.

Variable annuities. With these investments, you allocate your money among several choices, including some that resemble mutual funds. In effect, you can enjoy stock-market appreciation without paying taxes currently. The downside is that your account can lose value if you make the wrong investment choices, or if the broad stock market tumbles.

With either type of deferred annuity, there is no income tax as long as the money builds up. At the same time, your provisional income will not be increased, driving up taxes on your Social Security benefits. Instead, you can take cash when you want it so you control your tax obligations. You will have to contend with surrender charges (many insurance companies allow some free withdrawals each year) but you will not have to pay any penalty tax after you reach age 59-1/2.

Minimizing Munis

As you can see from the above description, tax-exempt income gets the same weight in the provisional income formula as taxable earned or investment income. Thus, your municipal bond income is effectively taxable—it contributes to your paying higher taxes on Social Security benefits.

For this and other reasons, when you reach the age when you are collecting Social Security, it may be time to sell your municipal bonds and muni funds. That might not be easy to do—retirees often like the idea of holding tax-exempt municipal bonds.

After-tax, the math of munis seems to be encouraging. Why own Treasury bonds or bond funds paying, say, 4% if you are in a high tax bracket? If you are in a 33% tax bracket, you would net only 2.68%; in a 35% bracket, you would net 2.60%. If you stretch for corporate bonds or bond funds, you might earn 4.5% (assuming you do not want to own junk bonds) but that interest is subject to state and local federal tax as well, which might drop your after-tax yield even lower.

Instead, you can buy muni bonds or funds (in-state munis, if you live in a high-tax state). You might earn 3%—and keep all 3%, thanks to the tax-exempt interest. After-tax, you keep more with munis.

That strategy probably makes sense while you are working. But after you retire and begin collecting Social Security, think again. Your tax bracket might drop, reducing the advantage of owning munis. If you are in a 15% tax bracket, in retirement you would net 3.4% with 4% Treasuries, more than you will receive from munis. Moreover, Treasuries are safer and more liquid than munis.

What's more, municipal bond income and Social Security benefits do not mix well, as noted. If you are receiving Social Security benefits, crunch your own numbers to see if it makes sense to own municipal bonds or bond funds. Assuming owning munis has become unappealing, what should you do?

If you do not need the cash flow, consider switching from munis to deferred fixed annuities. You may get a higher yield and the untaxed buildup will not cause your Social Security benefits to be taxed.

If you do need the income, consider shifting into Treasuries or corporate bonds, where the yields are higher than muni yields. After-tax, you might come out ahead.

As another alternative, shift money into stocks or stock funds. Unrealized appreciation will not be taxed; if you need money, you can get your hands on cash by selling shares. By keeping track of your portfolio you can sell shares at a taxable loss or at a gain taxed at only 15% (even 5%, if your retirement income is modest). The money you do not withdraw can stay in stocks, where your returns likely will exceed what you would have earned in municipal bonds.

Senior Support

Tax-reduction concerns may be important, not only to seniors, but also to their sons and daughters. In many families, middle-aged children help support parents or other elderly loved ones—and those costs can be extensive. To make this financial aid less of a burden, tax benefits may be claimed. What's more, minor adjustments in spending patterns or behavioral habits can result in major tax savings.

For example, a middle-aged son or daughter might be able to claim one or both parents as dependents. Each dependency exemption provides a $3,300 tax deduction in 2006, an amount that increases annually with inflation.

There is a catch, though. Upper-income taxpayers may not get any benefit from dependency exemptions. In 2006, tax savings are reduced for couples filing jointly with incomes over $225,750; those with incomes over $348,250 get no benefit at all from dependency exemptions.

Even if your income permits you to benefit from a dependency exemption, claiming a parent or other older relative is not easy. Certain tests must be met in order for someone to be a "qualifying relative," under the tax law:

Income: Your parent's income cannot exceed the dependency exemption amount: $3,300 in 2006. Fortunately, this amount refers to taxable income. For low-income parents, Social Security benefits are not taxable so this will not be a problem. Gifts, insurance proceeds, and tax-exempt interest also are excluded from the gross income calculation. (However, such items may have an impact on the support test, explained below.)

If your parent's gross income is just over the threshold, try to get below that amount. Bank CDs or bonds paying taxable interest might be switched to tax-exempt bonds or funds. Going from taxable bank interest to tax-exempt bond interest will not increase exposure to taxes on Social Security benefits.

Support: You must provide over half of a parent's support during the year. If your parent lives with you, put a fair rental value on the housing you provide, as well as the food, medicine, transportation, etc., that you pay for. If your parent does not live with you, money you pay towards rent or other housing costs can be included in your share of the support. You should keep track of this calculation throughout the year and make sure you wind up paying at least 51%. Urge your parent to defer year-end spending of personal funds if it is a close call.

Suppose, for example, your father lives with you this year. The cost of his food, clothing, transportation, recreation, health care, and similar necessities totals $6,000. Also suppose that you provide him with a room that you could rent to a third-party for $450 a month, or $5,400 a year. Thus, the total cost of his support is $11,400 this year: $6,000 plus $5,400. You must provide over half, or at least $5,701. Because you have provided $5,400 worth of lodging, another $301 in support puts you over this threshold.

Personal status: A dependent must be a U.S. citizen or a resident of North America.

Filing status: Your parent cannot file a joint tax return, unless the return is filed only to receive a refund for taxes paid.

Relationship: The person may be a relative (parent, step-parent, parent-in-law, grandparent, great-grandparent, aunt, or uncle). If "none of the above," he or she must be a full-time member of your household.

Multiply and Conquer

In some cases, all of the tests may be met but one: no taxpayer provides over half the support of a low-income senior. You might provide 30%, say, and your brother provides another 25% of your father's support.

In such situations, you and your siblings can agree to file Form 2120, a Multiple Support Declaration, on your tax return. To qualify, each signer must contribute at least 10% of the parent's support for the year, and the total must exceed 50%.

Assuming that the qualifications are met, the participating siblings can agree that one brother or sister will take the dependency exemption in a given year. The next year, another sibling may claim it, by agreement. However, a high-income sibling should not be included in the rotation because he or she will get little or no tax benefit, as explained above.

Taking the Credit

Another tax break may be available if you pay someone to care for your parent so you can work: you might be eligible for a dependent care tax credit. As much as $3,000 that you spend for home care and fees paid to an elder care day care center is eligible for the credit. Assuming your family income is over $43,000, the credit rate is 20% (lower incomes get a credit rate as high as 35%).

Suppose, for example, you and your spouse both work and your joint income is over $43,000. You spend more than $3,000 to have someone watch your widowed mother during the day.

Your tax credit would be worth $600: 20% of $3,000. If you hire someone to care for two people, that 20% credit can be applied to $6,000 in expenses, for $1,200 in tax savings.

What's more, you can claim this credit even if you do not meet the 50%+ support test, described above. Thus, this "dependent care credit" is not just for dependents. However, the qualifying relative must live with you for more than half the year.

What if your employer offers a flexible savings account (FSA) that covers dependent care? In most such plans, up to $5,000 can be contributed to the FSA and used for dependent care expenses, tax-free. If you are in such a plan, and parents are included as qualifying dependents, you probably will be better off using the FSA and foregoing the dependent care tax credit.

Healthier Deductions

Tax breaks also may result if you pay some or all of an elderly dependent's medical bills. Even if you cannot claim a relative as a dependent, you still may be able to deduct medical payments. You need to be able to meet all the dependency tests except for the $3,300 income limit, mentioned above. Also, for these expenses to qualify, you must pay the bills directly. Do not give money to a parent so that he or she can pay.

If your parent lives in your home, some capital expenses may be deductible, as long as the outlays must be made to treat a specific condition, at a doctor's written recommendation. Suppose your mother's doctor prescribes swimming to treat severe arthritis so you spend $28,000 on a home pool. Further suppose that before-and-after appraisals state that the pool increased your home's value by $20,000. The $8,000 difference may be taken as a medical deduction. Other examples of capital improvements that might lead to medical deductions include the installation of central air-conditioning for breathing disorders and providing wheelchair access.

Adding medical bills paid for a parent may put you over the 7.5%-of-income requirement for medical deductions. Suppose, for example, your income this year is $80,000—you need to spend over $6,000 (7.5% of $80,000) to deduct any medical expenses. If the total of your unreimbursed medical outlays is only $5,000, no deduction would be allowed.

In addition, say you provide over 50% of your widowed mother's support, including $4,000 you spend on her doctor bills, premiums for her Medigap and long-term care insurance, prescription drugs, etc. That brings your total to $9,000, allowing you a $3,000 medical deduction: $9,000 minus $6,000.

If several siblings participate in a multiple support agreement, as explained above, the one who will take the exemption in the current year should make the payments for the parent's medical bills. That will maximize deductible medical expenses for the year. The other siblings relinquish parent-related tax benefits for the year so any medical bills they pay will not be deductible.

There are some tax pitfalls to avoid, though. Money you spend on dependent care also may qualify as a medical expense but you cannot take the credit and the deduction for the same outlays. Thus, you should do the math to see which provides the greater tax benefit.

Go to the Head of the Household

If you are not married and you help to support a parent, you may claim head-of-household filing status. When you file as a head-of-household, you will owe less than you would as a single filer. To qualify, you must provide over half of your parent's housing costs or nursing home bills. Alternatively, your parent can live with you for over half the year. Various other tax rules are much more favorable for head-of-household filers than for singles so this can be a valuable tax break for those who qualify.

4

Estate Tax Planning

✦

Happy Outcomes

As of this writing, Congress is considering a "permanent" repeal of the federal estate tax. In reality, the words "permanent" and "federal tax" do not belong in the same sentence. No matter what Congress does, any future Congress may rescind, with new legislation. The bottom line is that planning for estate tax is extremely difficult. At the same time, it is extremely important. When assets pass to the next generation, significant taxes can be assessed under current law. Property, even a family business, may have to be sold, in order to pay the tax. So how can you plan for a tax that is both costly and complicated? By gearing your plan to current law, and building in sufficient flexibility so that you can adapt your plan as the law changes, to reduce the tax bill your heirs will have to face.

Current Affairs

Here is how the estate tax currently works. At your death, all of your assets (your home, your retirement plan, your investment portfolio, your coin collection, and so on) will be valued. The total value, net of debt, is considered to be your estate. Bequests to your spouse and to charity are tax-free. Thus, you can leave as much as you want to your spouse and to your favored causes, with no estate tax consequences.

Other bequests qualify for a specified exemption. In 2006, you can leave up to $2 million worth of assets before the federal estate tax kicks in. This exemption amount will increase to $3.5 million in 2009. In 2010, the federal estate tax is repealed...but in 2011 it returns, with a $1 million exemption.

It is extremely unlikely, to say the least, that such a bizarre law will remain on the books. Some lawmakers want to make estate tax repeal permanent. Others want to retain the federal estate, but with a larger exemption and lower rates.

Death and Taxes: Together Forever

Now, you might think that you don't have $10 million or even $5 million worth of assets, so estate tax planning is not necessary. That's not necessarily the case, though. In some parts of the U.S., anyone who owns a home and an IRA can be in estate tax territory. For many people, planning is still vital.

Moreover, current law provides that repeal of the estate tax will bring a complicated change in the income tax rules on inherited assets. In many cases, an heir's sale of inherited property would trigger a capital gains tax. If these so-called "carryover basis" rules ever go into effect, astute planning will be needed.

In addition, as the federal estate tax wanes, estate taxes are waxing in many states. You may well leave an estate that owes nothing to the IRS but does have to pay a sizable sum to New York, Massachusetts, or New Jersey.

Therefore, estate tax planning remains a necessity, for anyone who has accumulated significant assets. How can you proceed, though, in such an uncertain environment?

Update your documents. You should meet periodically with your professional advisors to make sure that your will, any trusts, and other estate planning documents are in accord with current law.

Re-evaluate traditional formulas: A common tactic has been to leave an amount equal to the estate tax exemption to the next generation, or to a trust for those beneficiaries. If you leave this type of language in place, millions of dollars might pass to your children while little is left for your surviving spouse.

Instead of making this type of bequest, put together a tax-efficient estate plan that will protect the interests of all parties. For example, you might leave all of your assets to your spouse but allow her to disclaim assets to your children (see below). Your spouse can decide what to retain and what to waive, based on the tax law in effect at that time as well as personal needs.

In addition, you should find out what your state's laws are, in this area, and work with your professional advisors to incorporate those laws into your estate planning. Moving to another state might be a good solution, in some cases.

Giveaway Game

Under current law, as mentioned, the estate tax exemption is $2 million. Suppose that Joan Smith reaches age 90 with $3 million worth of assets. She thinks it is unlikely she will take any more trips or entertain lavishly. Therefore, she figures that she will give $1 million worth of assets to her children. After that, she will die with only $2 million in her estate and owe no federal estate tax.

Unfortunately, that plan will not work because the federal estate tax is unified with a gift tax. In this example, Joan's executor would have to add back her $1 million in gifts when he files the estate tax return. The tax treatment would be the same as if Joan had died with a $3 million estate.

Nevertheless, there are ways to give away your estate without paying either gift or estate tax.

Annual exclusion. Each taxpayer is currently entitled to a $12,000 annual gift tax exclusion, which applies to an unlimited number of recipients. Suppose you have three children and four grandchildren. You can give some or all of these people up to $12,000 a year without incurring gift tax. The recipients owe no tax on the gift and you do not have to report it to the IRS, as long as you do not give away more than $12,000 per recipient. (The $12,000 limit increases periodically, to keep pace with inflation.)

This exclusion is very flexible: you do not have to give away the full $12,000 to each recipient and you can make gifts to anyone, not just to your relatives. In addition to the $12,000 exclusion limit, you can pay someone else's school tuition or medical bills without owing gift tax, if payments are made directly to the schools, doctors, hospitals, etc. Prepayment of several years of tuition bills is also allowed.

If you are married, the exclusion doubles. You and your spouse can each give $12,000 a year per recipient. Suppose, for example, you have $5 million in your own name while your spouse has nothing. You can make gifts to your spouse, tax-free, no matter how large the amount. Then your spouse can make $12,000 gifts to your son, daughter, etc.

Alternatively, you can make a gift of up to $24,000 and have your spouse consent to the gift. This means filing a federal gift tax return but you will not owe a gift tax as long as you do not exceed the $24,000-per-couple limit.

Single or married, you can repeat the process each year, making multiple gifts that use the annual gift tax exclusion. Over the years, you could remove substantial amounts from your estate, tax-free.

Lifetime exemption. Besides the annual exclusion, each taxpayer now has a $1 million exemption from gift tax. That is, you can give away up to $1 million, tax-free. Such gifts, though, eat into your estate tax exemption. If you use up your $1 million gift tax exemption and die when the estate tax exemption is $2 million, your estate tax exemption will be reduced to $1 million.

Nevertheless, it may pay to use up your lifetime exemption, even if it reduces your estate tax shelter. Once assets are given away, any future appreciation is out of your taxable estate. If you give away your $1 million beach house to your children, for example, no further tax will be due, even if the house is valued at $3 million when you die, many years later.

Out of Harm's Way

One strategy, then, is to give $12,000 to your son Brad, year after year, while your spouse also gives Brad $12,000 per year. There is a drawback to making outright gifts, though: a loss of control. Suppose you and your spouse give $120,000 to Brad over a five-year period, as above. If he is involved in a divorce, $60,000 could wind up in the hands of your ex-daughter-in-law.

Instead of outright gifts, you can make gifts to a trust. A typical arrangement might call for the creation of an irrevocable trust, with Brad as the trust's beneficiary. Assets given to the trust could be used for Brad's benefit but they probably would not be marital assets, subject to a divorce settlement. And they would be beyond the reach of any other creditors, too.

However, there are some issues to deal with if you would prefer to make gifts to trusts. Special care is needed if the gifts are to qualify for the annual gift tax exclusion.

Suppose you and your spouse fund a trust, as described above. Brad is the trust beneficiary. You and your spouse can give $24,000 worth of assets to the trust in 2006–$12,000 times two donors. To qualify for the gift tax exclusion, Brad (the beneficiary) must be notified of the gift. He must be given a time period in which assets can be withdrawn from the trust: $24,000 in this example. After the withdrawal window closes, the assets can remain in the trust and no gift tax will be assessed, provided the proper formalities have been followed.

Skip Without Getting Tripped

Suppose instead of giving the money to your son Brad, you give it to his daughter April. Now, the estate tax on this money can be skipped at Brad's death—the estate tax will not be owed until April's death, which might not be for many decades.

If you make such gifts, outright or in trust, they will be subject to a generation-skipping transfer (GST) tax. The same is true if you make bequests to a grandchild or great-grandchild.

The GST tax, therefore, is an extra level of transfer tax levied on bequests or gifts that skip at least one generation. In 2006, the GST tax rate is 46%. Fortunately, each individual now gets a $2 million exemption from the GST tax.

Thus, if you and your spouse transfer $2 million to a trust, you each can designate the use of $1 million worth of GST tax exemption. No GST tax will be paid.

Transfers to such trusts that exceed the $2 million-per-person ceiling will incur the GST tax, though. In addition, lifetime transfers over $1 million will be subject to gift tax, so the entire subject demands careful planning.

State of The Art

The current laws on estate, gift, and GST taxes stem from an act passed in 2001. In addition, the 2001 tax law hurt the states: according to one estimate, states stand to lose $100 billion in estate tax revenues over the next 10 years.

Before the 2001 tax act went into effect, federal law included a credit for state estate taxes, based on a formula. This credit went up to 16% while the highest federal estate tax rate was 55%. Thus, when a decedent's estate was in the 55% tax bracket, the executor would pay the state an amount equal to the 16% credit and the other 39% would go to the federal government. Similar splits were made for estates in lower federal estate tax brackets.

This credit has now been eliminated. The old system is scheduled to come back in 2011 but that may not happen if another tax law is passed in the interim, as many people expect. Thus, states have lost significant amounts of money and may not see any replacement coming from Washington. Some states have responded to this revenue shortfall by "decoupling" from the federal estate tax system. Rules differ from state to state but several states have passed new laws calling for the collection of the amount a state would have received, if the old credit had remained in place. Other states have lower estate tax exemptions than the federal government permits. For example, in 2006 the federal estate tax exemption is $2 million. New York, however, only recognizes a $1 million exemption; Massachusetts has an $850,000 exemption and in New Jersey assets over $675,000 are subject to estate tax. Some estates will owe tax to such states when they owe no federal estate tax.

Suppose, for example, Jack Baker dies in New York in 2006 with a $2 million estate. His estate would owe no federal estate tax but it would owe New York estate tax of $99,600.

Change of Scenery

What kind of planning might ease this state tax bite?

Gifts. In some states, the taxable estate is not adjusted for lifetime gifts, as is the case under federal law, explained above. For example, if Bob Williams has given away $2 million and dies with $5 million, he is treated as having a $7 million estate, by the IRS. Some states, though, do not follow the same add-back procedure, so Bob's estate would be taxed on a smaller amount. In fact, only four states currently have a gift tax: Connecticut, Louisiana, North Carolina, Tennessee. It is possible, moreover, that Connecticut might repeal its gift tax.

Bequests. For married couples, a basic strategy might call for the first spouse to die to leave some assets to the spouse and other assets to their children, outright or in trust. If you are concerned about state taxes, the children's bequest might be the largest amount that will not create a federal or state estate tax—$1 million in New York, for example. The balance of the estate can be left to the surviving spouse, tax-free, outright or in trust. You should be comfortable that an adequate amount is left to the surviving spouse.

Relocation. A relatively simple tactic is to move to another state. Florida, for example, does not impose estate tax and is unlikely to do so in the future. Relocating is especially appealing if you already have two homes, including one in a state where estate tax is not a major concern.

You should be aware, though, that changing "domicile" may require more than simply living in Florida for seven months a year. In addition, you should file a declaration of domicile in your new state, register to vote there, relocate your brokerage and bank accounts, change your driver's license, get new license plates for your car, and so on. You also might sell your house in your old state and replace it with a smaller home or apartment.

In other words, make a real move. If you go from a high-estate-tax state to one without steep death taxes, your heirs may wind up with substantial tax savings.

Learning how to "By-Pass" Estate Taxes

As mentioned, basic estate planning for married couples calls for the first spouse to die to leave some assets to their children, sheltered by the estate tax exemption, and some assets to the surviving spouse, because spousal bequests are untaxed. The challenge, though, is determining how much to leave to your kids and how much to your surviving spouse.

A classic solution is to leave a certain amount to a trust, naming your spouse as well as your children as beneficiaries.

This strategy:

1. uses your estate tax exemption;

2. removes those assets from your survivor's estate; and

3. provides your spouse with access to the funds, if necessary.

The type of trust described above is variously known as a bypass trust, a family trust, or a credit shelter trust. In addition, estate plans often include a marital trust—a trust where the surviving spouse is the sole beneficiary.

In the past, many estate plans have followed a formula. Whenever the first spouse dies, the estate tax exemption amount will go to a bypass trust while the rest will go to the surviving spouse in a marital trust. Under current law, though, this plan may shortchange your spouse.

Say that Walt Anderson dies in 2006 with a $2 million estate. If his plan calls for the exemption amount to go to a bypass trust, all $2 million will go to the trust, because that is the exemption amount in 2006. All of Walt's estate will go to the bypass trust, leaving nothing for his widow.

It is true, as stated above, that Walt's widow still can get money from the bypass trust. As long as her access to the trust funds is limited, the trust assets will not be in her taxable estate. Such provisions, though, probably will allow her needs to be met. Therefore, if your estate plan includes a bypass trust, you might want to be sure your spouse is among the beneficiaries, with the proper language in place.

However, even if your surviving spouse is a beneficiary of the bypass trust, her access to the trust funds will be restricted. There may be a psychological disadvantage, too, especially if your survivor must ask the trustee every time she needs a few extra dollars.

Spouse as trustee. One possible solution to this problem is to name your surviving spouse as the trustee or co-trustee of your bypass trust. This can give her more confidence and more control.

Spousal disclaimer. Another approach is to leave most or all of your assets to your spouse, outright or in trust. You can set up a bypass trust, too, which can be lightly-funded. After your death, your spouse can evaluate her financial situation and current tax law. Then she can disclaim an appropriate amount to the bypass trust, where those assets will not be subject to estate tax at her death. (See below for more on disclaimers.)

Limits on the bypass trust. Yet another strategy is to put a cap on how much of your estate can go into a bypass trust. Your estate plan might call for the exemption amount to go into a bypass trust, but not more than half of your estate. If you leave $2.4 million worth of assets, $1.2 million can go into the bypass trust, so it will not be taxed in your survivor's estate, while the other half can go to your spouse.

The cap might be expressed in dollars, instead. If your estate is $2.4 million and you put a $1 million cap on the amount that goes into a bypass trust, your surviving spouse would receive a $1.4 million inheritance.

Spousal bypass trust.

Alternatively, you might fund the bypass trust to the amount of the estate tax exemption and name your spouse as the sole beneficiary. This would help to provide for your spouse. Assets in a carefully drafted bypass trust would be out of the surviving spouse's estate. Your children might be secondary trust beneficiaries, to inherit after your spouse's death.

Other strategies might include funding a bypass trust with a minimum amount, to get those assets out of your survivor's taxable estate, and splitting your estate tax exemption between two bypass trusts, one for your surviving spouse and one for multiple beneficiaries.

The bottom line is that it may be necessary to plan for your own possible death (and your spouse's) as if death will occur right away. Each year, you can meet with your professional advisors to see if your plan is still valid. If not, you can make changes to comply with the any tax law that has gone into effect.

Sooner and Later

Besides a bypass trust, sophisticated estate plans also include a marital trust, for the benefit of the surviving trust. Often, these marital trusts are qualified terminable interest property (QTIP) trusts. QTIP trusts are especially valuable, if you are in a remarriage, with children from a previous marriage.

In a QTIP trust, all the assets will be solely for the benefit of the surviving spouse, during her lifetime. Typically, the trustee will be instructed to pay all trust income to the survivor and to distribute trust principal for specified purposes. Assuming a QTIP trust is properly structured, there will not be any tax imposed when you make a gift to such a trust or at your death.

At the death of your survivor, the assets remaining in the trust can pass to beneficiaries you name, perhaps your children from a prior marriage. At that point, estate tax may be due, depending on current tax law. Using a QTIP trust means that your children will have to wait—perhaps for many years—for an inheritance. Therefore, you might want to leave them other assets or buy insurance on your life, payable to your children.

Flex Plans

As noted, the 2001 tax law has made estate planning a puzzler. You might die when the estate tax exemption is $1 million, when it is $3.5 million, or when there is no estate tax at all. How can you cope with such uncertainty? The best solution is to build flexibility into your estate plan. After your death, your heirs can look at their personal finances and at current tax law. Then they can make the decisions that will lead to the lowest possible tax bill. Therefore, it is vital to educate your heirs so that they can act intelligently, when the time comes.

Heir Today, Gone In Nine Months

Well-informed heirs can execute a disclaimer strategy. An heir that you name in your will has nine months to waive an inheritance. This disclaimer might be a:

Full disclaimer. Your son Adam could waive his entire inheritance.

Partial disclaimer. Your daughter Beth might accept, say, your vacation home in the Hamptons but relinquish her claim to your investment real estate.

Fractional disclaimer. Your son Chris might accept, say, 50% ($500,000) of your IRA, for which he is the designated beneficiary, and disclaim the other 50% ($500,000).

What happens to any disclaimed assets? That depends on the terms of your will. Therefore, you should name backups.

For example, your will might state that any assets disclaimed by your spouse will be divided among your children. If your will does not specify recipients for such estate assets, they will be distributed as per state law, which may not be the arrangement you desire.

Too Much of a Good Thing

Why would anyone give up the right to an inheritance? To save taxes.

Say you leave $2 million to your daughter Debra. By the time you die, though, Debra is a wealthy investment banker. If she accepts the inheritance, she will receive money she does not really need and possibly increase her own estate tax bill. Instead, Debra can disclaim. Under your will, Debra's son Eric, your grandson, winds up with a $2 million inheritance. Those assets will not be subject to estate tax at Debra's death.

You should keep in mind, though, that when assets are disclaimed and the recipient is a grandchild or great-grandchild, the GST tax may be triggered, as explained above. Currently, each person has a $2 million exemption from this tax but larger amounts may be subject to this tax.

Disclaimers may be especially valuable in the case of retirement plans. Suppose that Paula Russell names her daughter Mindy as beneficiary of her IRA and names Mindy's children as contingent beneficiaries. If Mindy does not need Paula's IRA, she can disclaim. The grandchildren will then be the beneficiaries, with extra decades to stretch out minimum distributions while they benefit from tax-deferred compounding.

Grappling With Guesswork

As you can tell, the above disclaimer strategy may be valid under any system of estate taxation. The uncertainty of current law, though, may make disclaimers especially important. Neglecting to provide for disclaimers might be expensive for your heirs.

Suppose you anticipate that the estate tax will be repealed so you simply leave everything to your spouse. However, at your death, the estate tax is in effect and likely to remain so. Then your spouse's estate may have to pay a hefty tax bill in the future. If you have provided flexibility, your spouse could disclaim assets, which would pass to your children, using the current estate tax exemption to avoid a tax payment. This would reduce your spouse's taxable estate and the amount of estate tax your children eventually will owe. However, if assets pass to the children, your spouse will have no chance to benefit from them. Your spouse might be better off if your will provides for disclaimed assets to go into a bypass trust (see below).

The bottom line is that planning for estate tax has become extremely difficult. Tax law may change dramatically in the years before your death. Moreover, you cannot know whether your loved ones will be wealthy or needy in the future. Therefore, it is vital to build flexibility into your will. Give your heirs the chance to enjoy all of your assets but also build in a succession plan in case they can save taxes by passing on your wealth.

5

Asset Protection

◆

Cover Your Anatomy

The financial risks faced by seniors are by no means limited to catastrophic ill-ness, lengthy incapacity, or sinking stock markets. Winding up on the wrong end of an award for damages in a lawsuit could strip you of the net worth it took a lifetime to accumulate.

Nor is such an outcome so unthinkable. If you are at fault in a crippling auto accident, say, the victim could win a huge amount in court. The same is true if a visitor falls down the steps in your home. Professionals and corporate officers may face legal actions related to their careers, even after they have retired.

No single step can protect your personal assets from such threats. Neverthe-less, if you put together a coordinated program of asset protection, you can signif-icantly reduce your exposure.

Insist Upon Insurance

To begin, you should focus on a basic form of asset protection: covering your home, your cars, and the liabilities they might generate. Homeowner's insurance may be especially important today, after years of soaring home prices. You should be sure that you have a "replacement cost" policy rather than an "actual cash value" policy. With the latter, in case of damage you will receive the property's value, minus depreciation. Typically, that amount will be far less than it would cost you to replace or rebuild whatever is damaged.

As you would expect, though, a replacement cost policy will cost much more than an actual cash value policy. How can you trim your costs yet still maintain proper coverage? For homeowner's insurance, a higher deductible may be better than a low one. You will pay lower premiums if you do not expect your insurance to pay you back for every dollar you spend.

Today, many insurance companies recommend a deductible of at least $500. If you raise your deductible to $1,000, you may cut your premiums by up to 25%. With a higher deductible you will likely save money in the long run, even if you pay for the occasional broken window out-of-pocket, yet you will still have insurance against major disasters.

Another way to cut costs is to avoid over-insuring. Remember, the land under your house is not at risk from theft, windstorm, fire, etc. Therefore, you should not include its value in deciding how much homeowner's insurance to buy. If you do, you will pay a higher premium than necessary.

Making your home more secure also can lead to lower premiums. You need smoke detectors, for example; after you renovate or remodel, be sure your smoke detectors are re-connected.

Your insurance agent probably will be able to advise you on other steps you can take to make your home more resistant to natural disasters, and thus cut your premiums. Possible actions include adding storm shutters, reinforcing your roof, and buying stronger roofing materials. In addition, modernizing your heating, plumbing, and electrical systems can reduce the risk of fire and water damage.

Be wary of other risks, too. You might want to go beyond basic coverage and add earthquake insurance, which is not covered in most homeowner's policies. In many areas of U.S., earthquake insurance can be purchased through a relatively inexpensive rider to your homeowner's policy. You might need to buy separate flood insurance, too, depending on where you live.

In addition to insuring the house itself, your homeowner's policy also will cover its contents. A careful review of your homeowner's policy might show that you are paying too much and still not getting the coverage you need, when it comes to your possessions. Thus, you should check the limits in your policy and the value of your possessions at least once a year. You will want your policy to cover any major purchases but you do not want to spend money for coverage you do not need. If your five-year-old home entertainment system is no longer worth the $5,000 you paid for it, you will want to reduce or cancel your "floater" (extra insurance coverage for items whose full value is not covered by standard home-owner's policies) and reduce your premiums.

Limit Your Liability

Beyond insuring the value of your dwelling and its contents, homeowner's insurance also should include liability coverage. If your dog bites someone or a family member damages another person's property by accident, this coverage obligates your insurance company to defend you if you are sued, and to pay any damages, up to your policy limits. You will probably want to maximize this liability coverage; often, this means paying for $300,000 worth of liability coverage.

Similarly, you probably should maximize the liability coverage when you buy auto insurance. This liability insurance, which protects you if you cause damages or injuries in an auto accident, is actually made up of two different policies. Bodily injury insurance protects you if you cause personal injury to others while property damage insurance protects you if you cause damage to any physical property.

Auto liability coverage generally is expressed by three numbers, such as 50/100/25. These numbers mean that your coverage goes up to $50,000 for bodily injury caused to another person; up to $100,000 for bodily injuries caused to everyone in one incident; and up to $25,000 for property damage.

State laws will require a minimum level of auto liability insurance but you are better off paying more for more coverage. You might want to pay for liability coverage of 150/325/55, for example.

Other coverage also should be included in your auto insurance. Medical coverage, for example, covers medical expenses from crash injuries for you and your passengers, no matter who was at fault. Some states have so-called "no-fault" rules; in most of these states you can buy personal injury protection (PIP) to cover medical and rehabilitation expenses, work loss, funerals, and other expenses incurred by you, your passengers, or any pedestrians injured by your vehicle, regardless of who is at fault in the accident.

In addition, there are certain things you should look for in auto insurance. For example, if you have insurance on a car that you own or lease, is there coverage in case your teenaged children or grandchildren are driving and get into an accident? Make sure your policy will cover such situations.

Beyond liability insurance, you will probably want collision and comprehensive coverage for your cars. Collision coverage insures you against damage to your vehicle in an accident while comprehensive coverage insures your car against other physical damage from fire, theft, flood, and vandalism. Often, there is a deductible, ranging from $100 to $1,000, and the same advice applies here as to homeowner's insurance. By taking a higher deductible, you will lower the premium you will pay while still protecting against major damages. Indeed, if you have an old car with little value, you may want to drop collision and comprehensive insurance on that car altogether.

Certainly, you will want to protect yourself against major damage to a $25,000 or $35,000 car, just as you would want to protect a house that might be valued in the hundreds of thousands of dollars. Nevertheless, your major risk is on the liability side: if an injury occurs in your home or as result of an auto accident, you could face a judgment that runs into the millions of dollars.

Carry An Umbrella

In case of a serious accident, even carrying $300,000 or $325,000 worth of liability insurance would not be sufficient; bodily injury insurance might put a $300,000 limit on payments to a single injured person and a $500,000 cap on the total payments for all persons injured in one accident. Today, though, it is not impossible to wind up in a $2 million lawsuit if you are in an auto accident that causes personal injury. If you have nothing more than the standard $300,000 liability coverage, your insurance company will write a check for the $300,000 and walk away. Then you are on your own.

Excess liability ("umbrella") insurance will pick up after your auto insurance liability coverage runs out. (An umbrella also will supplement the liability coverage in your homeowner's policy.) If an auto accident results in a $2 million judgment, for example, and your auto liability coverage will pay $300,000, the other $1.7 million can come from an umbrella policy.

Generally, you should buy umbrella coverage for two times your net worth. With a $1 million net worth, for example, you might buy a $2 million umbrella policy. This type of policy also should protect you against claims for libel, slander, false arrest, wrongful entry, and invasion of privacy. Ideally, your umbrella policy will provide coverage if you face liability arising from your service on the board of a civic, charitable, or religious organization. Perhaps most important, an umbrella should pay for legal fees and defense costs—even if a lawsuit is frivolous, you still face the expense of defending yourself.

You need a certain amount of underlying insurance to get an excess liability policy. Once that underlying coverage is in place, it is generally inexpensive to add an umbrella. Typically, if you buy all three policies—home, auto, and umbrella from one insurer, you will qualify for lower premiums and assure yourself of seamless coverage.

Plan Preservation

If you should lose a damages award and your insurance coverage is absent or inadequate, your creditors naturally will want to seize your assets. Often, a tax-deferred retirement plan will be your most valuable asset, or among the most valuable. Therefore, protecting your retirement plan from creditors might be critical to your financial well-being.

Fortunately, there is some good news in that area. Under federal law, defined contribution and defined benefit plans are protected from creditors, judgments, and bankruptcy proceedings. Therefore, money that is held in a plan is virtually creditor-proof—only the plan participant's spouse, the IRS, and the plan itself can attach money held in the plan, under certain circumstances.

This protection may be powerful, indeed. In one case, a physician who filed for bankruptcy had accumulated nearly $2 million in a retirement plan. The physician's creditors challenged the exemption for retirement plans on the grounds that it was unfair. A court agreed with the creditors that the exemption was unfair but found that it must recognize the exemption. As a result, the physician eliminated all of his debts and walked away from bankruptcy with $2 million in his retirement plan. Had he invested it in a personal portfolio outside of a retirement plan instead, he would have lost the $2 million.

Thus, contributions to employer-sponsored retirement plans such as 401(k) plans and profit-sharing plans should be maximized, in order to enjoy creditor protection as well as tax deferral. Nevertheless, not all retirement plans enjoy this creditor protection. For example, a retirement plan is not protected under federal law if it covers only owners and owners' spouses. You need other participating employees. State laws, however, may provide some protection for such plans as they often provide broader protection than under federal law.

Immunize Your Investments

In addition to retirement plans, other investments may provide some creditor protection. Life insurance and annuities, for example, may be sheltered by state law. In such states, you might decide to invest through variable life insurance policies or variable annuity contracts rather than through mutual funds. Many variable life policies and variable annuity contracts offer a wide range of investments as well as tax deferral. (If you invest through variable life insurance and tap the policy carefully, taxes on investment income may be avoided altogether.)

So-called 529 college savings plans also might make the list of assets that creditors may not reach. Many states attach special statutory protections to accounts in their 529 plans. Some of these state laws protect a 529 account only from the beneficiary's creditors but most protect the account from any claims against the account owner and the beneficiary. These plans are relatively new, though, so it is uncertain what will happen if the account owner and/or the creditor is located outside the state granting such protection.

Real Estate Investors

Real estate investors also must be concerned with asset protection. If you own a house that you rent to tenants, you could suffer a severe financial loss if someone is hurt there and sues you for being negligent about maintaining the property.

Therefore, you might consider holding investment real estate in a limited liability company (LLC). Recently, LLCs have gained popularity because of their flexibility and tax advantages as well as their creditor protection. Consequently, real estate investments frequently are structured as LLCs so that claims generated on the property do not spill over onto investors' personal assets.

In fact, if you hold multiple real estate investment properties you may want to create a separate LLC for each one, rather than holding all properties in one LLC. With multiple LLCs, a tenant who suffers an injury at one of your properties would not have access to the assets of other properties you own.

Trust Tactics

While holding investment real estate inside an LLC may be a savvy move, another common approach—putting investment property into a revocable living trust—does not provide any creditor protection. All property held in such a trust is treated as the creator's personal assets, exposed to general creditors.

Although revocable trusts are not valuable for asset protection, traditional *irrevocable* trusts can provide shelter from creditors while offering tax reduction and financial support for loved ones.

Assets transferred to an irrevocable trust are out of the grantor's hands and thus beyond the reach of the trust beneficiary's creditors. Depending on your choices of trustee and beneficiaries, your family may continue to enjoy use of the assets. Suppose, for example, you transfer assets to an irrevocable trust created for the benefit of your spouse and children. Subsequently, your creditors may have a difficult time attaching the trust assets. (The issue of fraudulent conveyance must be considered. According to the Uniform Fraudulent Transfers Act, any property transferred for the purpose of avoiding creditors represents a fraudulent transfer and can be set aside. For a wealth protection game plan to be effective, it must be implemented before there is the known threat of a lawsuit.)

To keep assets from creditors, irrevocable trusts should have "spendthrift" provisions, which restrict the trust beneficiaries' rights to transfer their interest in the trust. Such spendthrift provisions also serve to prevent trust beneficiaries from making foolish agreements regarding future distributions. In such trusts, beneficiaries cannot borrow against their trust interest or otherwise pledge future payments. Thus, creditors are prevented from reaching trust assets. Some states automatically apply spendthrift provisions while others require specific language.

Once spendthrift provisions are in place, the protection may be very strong, indeed. In one recent case, an assault victim won a civil judgment against the perpetrator. The defendant was the beneficiary of a trust established by his grandmother, with typical spendthrift language. In this state (New Hampshire), the only exceptions to spendthrift provisions are trusts where the grantor is the beneficiary and fraudulent conveyances. Thus, a court ruled that creditors (the assault victim, in this case) could not reach the trust assets.

This example does not imply that the people you name as beneficiaries of a trust will commit egregious acts. However, it does show that a properly-structured irrevocable trust can offer substantial creditor protection.

Present Perfect

As the above discussion implies, if you want to transfer assets to younger relatives, gifts in trust make a practical alternative to large outright gifts. Suppose, for example, Bill Collins is concerned about future estate taxes. He is advised that he can reduce his taxable estate by giving $1 million worth of assets to his children and not have to pay gift tax.

However, Bill's daughter Melanie is a surgeon while his son Gil is a corporate officer. Giving each of them $500,000 would expose that money to his children's creditors. On the other hand, giving that $1 million to a trust and naming his children as trust beneficiaries would present a substantial barrier to creditors of Bill, Melanie, or Gil.

Avoid Splitting Headaches

Such transfers of assets in trust also can keep wealth in the family in case of a future divorce. If assets are given outright to children and those children later are divorced, those assets may be subject to a property settlement. Assets held in trust, though, can remain in place.

Suppose, for example, you transfer assets to a trust for your daughter Kim—a few years later, Kim's marriage breaks up and her husband wants some of the trust fund, as part of the settlement. It is likely that a court would look at the pattern of distributions from the trust and make an award on that basis, which would preserve most of the trust assets.

If you are considering gifts in trust, discretion may be prudent. That is, you might want to give the trust a great deal of leeway in deciding how much to distribute to beneficiaries. The more that is required to be distributed, the more that may be available to creditors, including divorcing spouses.

Transfers to trusts may protect assets not only for your children but also for your grandchildren and other descendants. So-called "dynasty" trusts are designed to be in effect for many decades. Beneficiaries, who might include your spouse, children, grandchildren, and others, can receive distributions for health care, education, housing, business startups, and other crucial needs. Yet the assets in a properly-designed dynasty trust will avoid future estate taxes as well as claims from creditors, divorcing spouses, etc.

Keep in mind, though, that naming grandchildren and other future descendants may trigger the generation-skipping transfer (GST) tax, which is essentially an extra layer of estate tax. The GST tax need not wreck a transfer to a dynasty trust but it does call for thoughtful planning by a knowledgeable professional.

Trust-Worthy Travel

While most irrevocable trusts offer considerable asset protection, some states have taken extra steps to offer "asset protection trusts." Alaska, for example, has ratified trust rules that protect assets from creditors while still providing trust creators with some access to the trust funds. That is, if you transfer some of your assets to a trust, out of the reach of creditors, a friendly trustee could distribute these assets back to you in case of an emergency. To qualify, some of the trust assets must be held in an Alaska institution, with at least one Alaska trustee. Other states, including Delaware, Colorado, Missouri, Nevada, and Rhode Island, have passed similar laws regarding "self-settled" trusts.

Domestic asset protection trusts are still relatively new so it is difficult to determine whether they will be effective in repelling creditors. Some people feel that assets may be best protected if they are moved from the U.S. legal system to a jurisdiction that discourages creditors.

In recent years, several offshore jurisdictions have passed trust laws that may discourage creditors. They are positioning themselves as "asset protection havens," where creditors have extra hurdles to clear. Often, the assets can remain in the U.S. even though title to those assets is offshore. Just having assets in a foreign trust may discourage some plaintiffs (and their attorneys) from proceeding against you: they will seek easier pickings. Indeed, the thought of pursuing a claim in an unfriendly distant court may cause some creditors to settle on favorable terms rather than pursue claims. However, the expenses involved in setting up such a plan are significant while some people are leery of offshore dealings.

Title Games

You do not have to create trusts in order to protect your net worth. Another basic asset protection measure is to review property ownership. Depending on how your assets are held, creditor protection may be increased.

You should know state laws, because they vary. In many states, there may be ways to increase creditor protection by transferring ownership among family members. Often, this is a crucial issue for married couples.

Most couples title the bulk of their assets in their joint names. Unfortunately, in some states, if assets are held in this manner, a creditor may be able to force the sale of the property in order to collect the judgment and be entitled to half of the proceeds. In other states, however, the creditor will not be able to force the sale. Instead of joint ownership, if one spouse is at a significantly greater risk of being sued, it may make sense to transfer assets to the other spouse's name.

For example, if one spouse has substantial exposure to creditors because of business or professional circumstances, the majority of the family assets might be held by the homemaker spouse. (Such tactics might not be effective in community property states such as California but another family member may be given assets if a transfer to a spouse is not appropriate.)

The conventional wisdom holds that spousal transfers can be disastrous if the client is in a shaky marriage that later ends in a divorce, but that may not be the case. If you become divorced in a separate property state, the fact that you transferred your interest in marital property (acquired during the marriage) to your spouse will have little affect on how property is split upon divorce. Non-marital property, including property acquired prior to the marriage and inherited property, should remain segregated from marital assets and be treated with more care.

Action Plans

No matter what measures you take to protect your assets, no strategy offers absolute security. It is always possible that a debtor will assert that the change of ownership was done primarily to avoid an obligation and thus should be annulled.

The concept of fraudulent conveyance, described above, dates back 400 years, when an English debtor sold sheep to a friend, yet continued to possess and shear the sheep. In 1601, the whole deal was ruled a fraud and the debtor wound up being sheared: he lost his sheep. The former sheep owner lost the case because assets were transferred to avoid an existing debt. The same concept applies to transfers made after an act already has been committed (an auto accident, say) that likely will lead to a claim for damages. Thus, transfers will move assets out of danger only if they are made before there are actual or potential creditors. Timing counts, too. Transfers to a trust that occurred five years ago are more likely to be respected than a transfer made one day before a lawsuit was filed.

Asset retention also counts. You are less likely to be charged with fraudulent conveyance if you leave some assets within creditors' reach, rather than put all of your holdings in trusts, limited partnership, spousal ownership, etc. For example, if you have $2 million in net worth, do not try to shelter all $2 million. To reduce your chances of running into trouble, keep, say, $500,000 in play while sheltering the other $1.5 million. (Of course, the $500,000 you leave exposed might be the assets you are most willing to part with, such as illiquid minority interests in real estate ventures.)

Fine Points

Before you undertake any asset protection strategy, find out what costs will be involved. Some of the techniques described in this chapter may involve upfront and ongoing expenses.

Be aware of the tax angles, too. Transferring substantial amounts of assets might trigger a gift tax. On the other hand, such transfers remove the assets from your taxable estate as well as any appreciation enjoyed by those assets after the transfer.

In addition to tax law, you should know your state's law, as regards asset protection. Some states have broad lists of assets that are exempt from creditors' claims. In some states, for example, your "homestead" is off-limits to creditors, no matter how valuable it is.

In such states, if you prepay your mortgage, you are putting assets where they cannot be touched. Another strategy is to buy a super-expensive house. It even may be worth relocating to such a state, if you are truly determined to protect the wealth you have managed to accumulate.

Finally, be prepared to justify your actions. In case a dispute comes to court, you should not say that you entered into transactions in order to protect assets from creditors. Instead, you should have another credible reason—such as reducing estate tax or providing security for your family.

Ultimately, these techniques are designed to motivate potential creditors to settle on favorable terms, in case of a dispute. The sooner walls are erected and the sturdier they are constructed, the less likely adversaries will be eager to scale them.

6

Long-Term Care

✦

Hope For The Best But Plan For The Worst

The good news? We are living longer. Life expectancy continues to increase among Americans. About 40% of the people living to age 65 are projected to live to be 90 by the middle of this century, compared to 25% in 1980. That means lower premiums for life insurance, less pressure to take required distributions from your IRA, and more time for seniors to spend with loved ones or to pursue favored pastimes.

The bad news? We are living longer. The older you are, the less likely you will be able to live independently. An AARP study has found that 83% of individuals 85 and older have a chronic condition or disability for which they might need assistance. Some day, someone may have to help you do things you once could do on your own, whether that help is provided at home or in another setting.

In the language of the growing industry that has developed to serve seniors, many people will need *long-term care*. This expression does not necessarily refer to medical care, which you might get in a hospital or a rehab center. More often, it refers to custodial care: having someone help you to eat, get around, and perform personal functions you no longer can manage on your own. As the term suggests, the need for this care may last for many years.

Who will provide this care? Your spouse will be getting older and might need care for him or herself. Your son or daughter and their spouses may live hundreds of miles away; even if they are close at hand, they likely have other things to do with their busy lives. They might call regularly and stop by occasionally, but it is unlikely that relatives will be able to provide all the care you need, for an extended time period. Indeed, obtaining and paying for long-term care has become the single most important issue facing the elderly population in the U.S.

Paying the Price

The short answer is that you will have to pay someone (now known as a caregiver, of course) if you need long-term care. Such services are expensive today and certain to go much higher tomorrow. The average rate for a private room in a nursing home is $192 a day, or about $70,000 a year, according to a 2004 survey by Metropolitan Life Insurance Co. (The cost of a shared room averaged nearly $62,000 a year.) Near-term, nursing-home costs are projected to rise by 5.6%-5.9%, according to the federal government's Centers for Medicare & Medicaid Services.

At a 6% rate of increase, costs double in about 12 years. Thus, the average nursing home might cost around $140,000 a year in 2016, and $280,000 per year in 2028!

And that is the average. In some areas of the Northeast, nursing home costs are 50% higher (or more) than the national average. In Stamford, Connecticut, for example, private nursing home rooms averaged $331 per day, or over $120,000 per year.

Maybe, you say, a nursing home will not be necessary. You will be able to stay at home and pay people to come in. That might be true, but home-health aides charge $18 an hour. At 10 hours a day, that is almost as much as a nursing home will cost.

If you need more tending, home care will be more expensive than a nursing home. Besides, the cost of home health care is forecast to rise even more steeply than nursing home care.

Responsibility Begins At Home

The bottom line is that long-term care is likely to be an expensive proposition for you and your family. Where, then, will the money come from? To start with, out of your pocket, or out of the pockets of loved ones willing to provide some support. In 2002, a Senate special committee on the aging found that 23% of all long-term care costs were paid out of pocket.

Pockets are only so deep, though. The average nursing home stay is 2.4 years, which means some stays are shorter but some are even longer. If you have to fund an extended stay in a nursing home or in your own home, at upwards of $100,000 per year, you likely will run low (or out) of money.

Premiums for Protection

Forewarned is forearmed. If you know that there is a risk you might have to transfer your life's savings to nursing home operators and home-health aides, you might insure against that risk. Indeed, many people are following that path of thought. Long-term care (LTC) insurance is the fastest-growing type of insurance in the U.S. today, as the size of this market increases by 20% per year. Purchasers include not only seniors but their middle-aged sons and daughters. The more middle-aged people have to care for aging relatives, the more they realize what a burden it can be, so the more likely they will pay for LTC insurance.

Cost savings are not the only reason to buy LTC insurance, for you or for a parent. Even if you have the money to pay for care, at home or in a facility, you may not have the time to figure out what care is needed and monitor it regularly. Increasingly, insurance companies are including "care coordination" with LTC policies, meaning they will help with the necessary arrangements. Insurers are presenting these policies to seniors' children as a way to preserve their lifestyle.

A Look at LTC Insurance

As you can imagine, providing years of custodial care might cost hundreds of thousands of dollars. This may be an enormous burden, especially for a married couple if one spouse must maintain a residence while the other requires care in a nursing home. Even if long-term care can be provided at home, the amounts paid to qualified people may be immense.

To reduce this exposure, LTC insurance may be desirable. A policy that pays, say, $100 per day would contribute over $36,000 per year towards the cost of needed care. Of course, buying a policy that pays $200 per day will provide even more support but would be more expensive.

If you are considering the purchase of LTC insurance, it is important to buy an adequate amount of coverage but not to overpay for excess benefits; and it is vital to acquire a policy that will pay for at-home as well as nursing-home care if certain activities of daily living (ADLs) cannot be performed. Beyond the amount and the conditions of coverage, though, you should know how the different types of LTC policies work.

Indemnity policies are traditional for LTC coverage. You might buy a policy that will pay a daily benefit of, say, $100 per day if you need care. (This need may be triggered if you suffer from failing mental or physical capabilities.) Once the need is certified and you receive care, the policy would pay the stated benefit of $100 per day, perhaps increased by an inflation adjustment.

Reimbursement policies have been gaining ground recently. These policies resemble health insurance coverage because they pay providers for services rendered, rather than pay a fixed amount to the policyholder. Generally, reimbursement policies are more affordable than indemnity policies, which mean you can purchase a greater LTC benefit for the same premium dollars.

Either way, LTC policies can be complex, with many riders and exclusions. However, some insurance companies are attempting to simplify things for consumers. There are fewer choices that have to be made with these policies, to reduce complexity. A company might offer policies with common features, such as a 30-day waiting period and full benefits for home health care. Once those constants are in place, a few variations might be offered. For example, one policy might be top-of-the line, with a $180 daily benefit, payable for life, compounded to keep up with inflation. Another policy might be bare-bones, with a $90 daily benefit, paid for no more than two years, and no inflation protection. A third could fall in the middle.

Mending Misconceptions

There are many misconceptions about long-term care. People may think they are covered by Medicare or by a medical insurance plan, which usually is not the case. According to the Senate Subcommittee on Aging, only 14% of LTC costs are covered by Medicare. In general, Medicare pays for *medical* care, not custodial care. So-called Medigap insurance policies, designed to supplement Medicare, provide very limited benefits for nursing care.

Another misconception is that LTC insurance should be bought late in life. According to the American Health Care Association, someone who buys LTC insurance at age 65 would pay about twice as much per year as would be paid for a similar policy, bought at age 55. Someone who waits until age 79 would pay around four times as much, per year, as a 65-year-old would pay. An LTC policy bought at age 56 might cost $1,500 per year while a similar policy bought at age 69 might cost $4,500. Long-term, it is less expensive to buy early and you will have additional years of coverage.

Moreover, people who wait to buy this coverage may incur certain health conditions that will prevent them for acquiring LTC insurance at all. The younger and healthier you are when you purchase LTC insurance, the lower the cost will be.

New Direction

From a practical point of view, the best time to buy LTC insurance may be after you are finished paying college bills. The money you have been sending in that direction might be used for LTC premiums.

Be sure to buy a policy with inflation protection, especially if you are in your 50s or 60s. Many people do not collect on their LTC policies until they are in their 80s. Two decades of 5% price hikes can multiply costs by more than two-and-a-half times. If you buy, say, a $150-a-day benefit today, it might be inadequate 20 years from now. An inflation rider will boost the benefit you can receive.

An LTC policy with an inflation rider can be expensive. Choosing a 60- or 90-day waiting period might help you save on premiums, as compared to a policy that pays off right away. However, going to an even longer waiting period will not save you much, compared with the extra costs you might incur while waiting for the coverage to kick in.

In Sickness or In Health

Naturally, insurance companies do not want to sell LTC insurance to people who are en route to the nursing home. Therefore, they will check on your health before they will provide coverage: this process is called underwriting. Different insurance companies, though, do not all have identical underwriting policies. Some are more tolerant of certain conditions than others. Working with an experienced agent can help you find the best insurer, for your particular health condition. At many companies, a streamlined underwriting process makes it easier to buy LTC insurance. Some insurers use trained nurses to interview applicants by phone; they claim they get better and faster information than they would get by relying upon the applicants' doctors. Using nurses instead may take weeks off the time until an application is approved.

Squeeze Play

Insurance companies may be trying to make LTC coverage simpler and quicker to obtain but they have not won unanimous praise for their efforts. Certain insurers have raised rates in recent years, straining the budgets of elderly policyholders. Today's problems, in fact, stem from yesterday's mistakes.

Some LTC policies previously offered low premiums, liberal benefits, and permissive underwriting. With this approach, many companies ran into trouble. As a result, you have to be careful about LTC policies. You might want to buy a policy only from a top-rated company, one with assets in the billions of dollars. Such a company may be leery of adverse publicity from rate increases. Buying from an insurer with financial strength also can help you feel confident that the company will be around when it is time to pay out benefits.

Generally, you should not shun an insurance company that has raised rates on LTC policies issued 10 to 20 years ago. Back then, companies did not know what they were doing with LTC insurance. In the past 10 years, though, companies have known a lot more about these policies—or they should have. A premium increase on a policy issued since then can be seen as warning sign of poor management...and a red flag indicating a company you might want to avoid.

In addition, choosing a "10-pay option" may help you avoid unpleasant surprises in future years. With a 10-pay rider, you fully pay for an LTC policy in 10 years. Although this increases the annual premiums, it cuts down on the number of years you will pay premiums. With a 10-pay policy, moreover, you will avoid potential premium increases that may take effect in subsequent years.

Making LTC Insurance Less Taxing

Tax breaks may effectively make LTC insurance more affordable. The Health Insurance Portability and Accountability Act (HIPAA) of 1996 provided for tax benefits for buyers of policies with certain features. Consequently, about 90% of the policies sold now are "tax-qualified."

Between tax-qualified and nonqualified LTC policies, the former offer two tax advantages:

1. Premiums may be deductible, up to certain limits, depending on the age of the insured individual;

2. Benefits received under tax-qualified LTC policies generally will not be taxable.

In order to qualify for these tax breaks, LTC policies must meet certain standards. Insurance benefits can be paid only if the insured individual is unable to perform at least two of these activities: eating, bathing, dressing, getting out of bed, using the toilet, and continence. Moreover, a licensed health care professional must certify that these conditions will last for at least 90 days.

Those are the standards for new policies. All LTC policies bought before 1997 are grandfathered so they qualify for the two tax breaks listed above. If you have such a policy, do not let it lapse without careful consideration.

Taking Care of Business

If you purchase an LTC policy on behalf of a parent who is not a dependent, you are not entitled to a medical expense deduction for those outlays. However, there are circumstances in which you may be able to get substantial deductions for LTC insurance:

- If you are self-employed you can treat the premiums for LTC insurance the same as health insurance premiums, for tax purposes. In this situation, you can deduct 100% of the premiums you pay, up to the amount of your self-employment income. The same is true for owners of S corporations and limited liability companies. Those deductions are subject to the age-based limits mentioned above.

- If you run a company as a regular C corporation, the corporation can deduct premiums paid for LTC insurance for yourself and for your spouse while no taxable income is recognized. What's more, you do not have to provide this coverage for your other employees.

Middle Ground

As mentioned, tax-qualified LTC policies pay benefits only if the insured individual cannot perform some basic activities. Increasingly, though, seniors who cannot live independently are moving into assisted living facilities (ALFs), where they receive some care but not full-time help with their daily living.

Will LTC insurance pay for assisted living? Maybe, but maybe not. These policies generally pay for care, not for living expenses, so a policy that covers assisted living may pay only part of the monthly bill. In some cases, LTC insurance will not pay at all if you are in an ALF.

You should review any policy, especially home-health-care-only policies, nursing-home-only policies, or any policy issued before 1990. If assisted living coverage is not included, ask the insurer if that coverage can be added, and, if so, how and at what cost.

One problem: many residents in ALFs, especially those with cognitive problems, may not be physically incapacitated enough to trigger benefits under most

LTC insurance policies. Thus, you might move to an ALF, thinking that your LTC insurance will pay for the care, only to find out your claim is denied. If you are determined to fight this battle, make sure that you have the ability to pay out-of-pocket not only during the waiting ("elimination") period, but also during any claims denial and appeal process.

This problem arose for Mary Harris, as we will call her, who lived in an ALF. She had an LTC policy that was paying a daily benefit. At one point, though, the insurance company notified her that she had reached the maximum amount payable, so benefits would stop. The problem, it turned out, was a matter of terminology. This was an old policy, and the definitions were vague as to what would be considered "home care" and what would be coverage for a "personal care facility." Mary contacted her insurance agent, who recommended an elder care attorney, who helped draft a letter to the insurance company. The episode ended with the daily benefit continuing and the insurer agreeing to clarify its policy definitions. The lesson? You should consult with a knowledgeable agent when considering LTC insurance. Find out whether assisted living is covered, at what cost, so you can make an informed decision.

Another form of "LTC insurance" also is available, one that covers assisted living. Some ALFs are in complexes known as "continuing care retirement communities". In essence, these centers offer residents the opportunity to move from independent living to assisted living to institutional care, if and when more care is needed. The concept sounds fine but the required upfront cost can be a major issue. Some of these centers charge $250,000 upfront; others have lower initial outlays but higher monthly charges. Make sure you know all the costs as well as the services you will receive, before making any decisions.

In Good Company?

About 20% of large U.S. companies offer LTC insurance to employees and more employers are expected to follow. Such group coverage can be valuable to employees who are in poor health. Outside of group plans, almost 20% of those who apply for LTC insurance are rejected for health reasons. Within a group plan, employees may be guaranteed coverage or face only minimal health questions.

However, group LTC coverage is not always a good deal, especially if you are in good health. With group coverage, healthy employees wind up subsidizing those in poor health so people without medical problems might do better on their own. A healthy 55-year-old may be able to buy a solid LTC policy for around $500 per year, as an individual, while that same person could pay $750 a year in a group plan, for comparable coverage.

What's more, with a group plan you are limited to the options chosen by your employer and you may be vulnerable to policy increases approved by your employer.

The Right Combination

Whether offered through an employer or available for individual purchase, LTC insurance has a flaw in the minds of many consumers. You might pay tens of thousands of dollars in premiums, over the years, and wind up needing little or no custodial care. If so, few benefits will be collected, in relation to the premiums paid.

Seniors who are uncomfortable with this possibility might want to choose from a number of combination products on the market. For example, some variable annuities will pay a monthly benefit in case care is needed. A variable annuity might not be a full long-term care solution but it does provide some protection and increased awareness of insurance as a solution to long-term care. If you never need long-term care, you will still have the extra retirement income an annuity can provide.

Similarly, some life insurance policies provide lifetime access to the death benefit for long-term care in case of need. That is, if you have a $200,000 life insurance policy, you might draw down $90,000 while you are alive, for long-term care, leaving only $110,000 for your beneficiary after your death. Again, if care is not needed your beneficiary will receive the full $200,000 death benefit. Some people buy this type of life insurance policy because they are not comfortable with the concept of long-term care, which is "use it or lose it," as described above. If you buy life insurance with a long-term care rider, you know that the premiums you pay will provide a benefit for someone (yourself or a beneficiary you have named), at some time. Such life insurance policies can be single-life or second-to-die. In the latter case, the death benefit will not be paid until two people, usually a married couple, have both died. If a second-to-die policy has an LTC rider, both spouses will have another source of funds to pay for long-term care.

Yet another strategy may be to use life insurance in a different way. Here, you would buy straight life insurance, with no long-term care coverage. Even if you must pay large amounts for long-term care, depleting your assets, your heirs will one day receive the insurance proceeds. This approach is known as wealth replacement because wealth lost to long-term care costs can be replaced by life insurance.

Last Resort

While many people pay for their own long-term care and a few (an estimated 6% of seniors) have LTC insurance, private funds and insurance proceeds may eventually run out. In those situations, people might look at Medicaid as the solution. Medicaid, a federal-state welfare program that pays medical bills for the impoverished, picks up nearly half of the nation's nursing home tab.

Thus, Medicaid has become "nursing home insurance" for many Americans. If you have few assets and little income, you can qualify for Medicaid, which will pay if you go into a nursing home. In general, applicants are not allowed to own much beyond a house, a car, and a few thousand dollars.

Some middle-class Americans become "artificially poor" in order to qualify for Medicaid. They transfer nearly all of their assets to family members, and then apply for Medicaid as poverty cases. To make this process work, there are rules you need to follow.

As a result of recent federal legislation, when you apply for Medicaid, you must list all transfers (gifts, below-market sales) within the previous 60 months, whether made outright or to a trust. Previous law provided a 36 month "lookback" period for outright gifts. Transfers made within this 60 month "lookback" period create a "penalty" period, i.e., a period of months that you do not qualify for Medicaid to pay for nursing home coverage. Unfortunately, under this new law, the penalty period does not start to run until the day you are in a nursing home and otherwise financially qualify for Medicaid—but for this penalty period. Under old law, the penalty period began when the transfer was made.

The Waiting Game

At the time of this printing, elder law and long term care planners were still trying to understand the full impact of this new Medicaid provision and to develop appropriate planning strategies. Clearly the only sure-fire option is to transfer assets and wait 60 months before applying for Medicaid. In such a case, there will be nothing to report and no problems qualifying—assuming your assets are otherwise below the poverty line. Another potential strategy that may see increased significance is the purchase of a commercial annuity or use of a private annuity to change what was otherwise an available resource into an income stream.

Does it make sense for you to become impoverished so Medicaid will pay any future nursing home bills? Not if you are still relatively young and healthy. After such a transfer, you will become dependent upon your loved ones for financial support.

However, as you grow older, you are more likely to need nursing home care. At this stage of your life, you can either:

- Hold onto your assets and risk losing most or all of them to a nursing home or a series of home-health aides;

- Buy LTC insurance, if you can get it at an affordable price; or

- Transfer assets to loved ones and apply for Medicaid once the waiting period is over. Then, Medicaid will pay the nursing home bills. (If you have to go into a nursing home sooner, family members can pay the expenses in the interim.)

Transferring assets from one spouse to another may not work because one spouse cannot have more than a certain amount of assets (about $75,000 in many states) in order for the other spouse to qualify for Medicaid. Often, Medicaid transfers are made to grown sons or daughters.

If you think you might want to transfer assets in the future, to become eligible for Medicaid, your long-term care plan should include powers of attorney. In case you become incompetent, the agent you name can make the transfers indicated.

Trust Tactics

Rather than outright transfers, there may be situations in which you will be willing to incur the legal fees of making transfers to a trust. That would be a good choice, for example, if you wish to transfer assets to your son Bob, who is a spendthrift, or to your daughter Carol, who is in a marriage that may wind up in a divorce. Bob and Carol will be better off if the assets you wish to transfer are in the hands of a reliable trustee.

Tax considerations may play a role, too. Suppose you are giving away appreciated assets. The recipients likely will owe capital gains tax when they sell those assets. However, using a carefully-structured trust to receive those assets might minimize that tax.

In another situation, you may want to provide for someone who is disabled. Outright gifts may not be appropriate but a trust can provide long-term security for the trust beneficiary. (See Chapter 10 for a discussion of "special needs" trusts.)

What's more, gifts to a disabled child or a trust created for that child's benefit do not count as transfers for the purpose of determining Medicaid eligibility. You can make such a transfer today and apply for Medicaid tomorrow. To qualify as a disabled child, he or she must meet Social Security's definition of disability: not able to do meaningful amounts of work because of a physical or mental condition.

Patients Need Patience

Even if Medicaid planning is on your agenda, do not rush to give away so many assets that you bring yourself down to the Medicaid level right away. If you will need nursing home care one day, you will be better off entering as a "private-pay" resident (paying the full posted rate) rather than as a Medicaid participant. In theory, there should be no discrimination among nursing home residents. In reality, though, private-pay patients are on the upper rung: they are more valued by the nursing homes.

LTC insurance, too, is valued by these homes. Even if the policy will only pay benefits for one or two years, to a nursing home administrator that is one or two years of solid revenues. If people have insurance that will pay in full for three years, nursing homes are happy to bring them in.

Savvy planning might call for people who need to be in a nursing home to enter as private patients, paying their own way or using insurance benefits. Patients have more of a selection among nursing homes when they enter as private payers, too. With Medicaid, you have to go where there is a bed available, even if that bed is far from friends and family.

LTC insurance benefits or personal assets may run out, though. If a nursing home resident becomes eligible for Medicaid, and the nursing home participates in the Medicaid system, he can stay in the familiar place. Nurses and other employees have no clue when a resident goes from private-pay to Medicaid so there probably will not be a change of care for someone who switched over to Medicaid.

There is a trap, though, if you choose a nursing home that does not participate in Medicaid. Take the case of Ellen King, as we will call her, who needed to go into a nursing home. She had some assets so she could pay privately—she went into a desirable nursing home. That nursing home was so desirable, in fact, that it raised prices tremendously and refused to take Medicaid patients. Ellen's advisors suggested she move to another facility. The second nursing home participates in Medicaid so Ellen was able to stay there after her money ran out and she went on public assistance. If she had remained in the first nursing home, spending down her assets, she would have had to move to another nursing home that participates in Medicaid, at a time when she had little or no choice of facilities.

Rush Job

If you need to go into a nursing home and no preparations have been made, what can you do?

- Arrange for admission to a high-quality nursing home (one that participates in Medicaid) on a private-pay basis.

- Then implement an asset transfer program, leaving yourself enough assets to pay nursing home bills until you can qualify for Medicaid.

Although such strategies can preserve some assets for your loved ones, you should not wait until the last minute to prepare for long-term care. Instead, decide right away if you will pay for care (1) out-of-pocket; (2) via LTC insurance; or (3) by going on Medicaid. Then take the steps necessary to implement your plan.

7

Indispensable Insurance

◆

Cover Your Health and Your Life

As discussed in Chapter 6, seniors need to consider whether they want to buy insurance that will help pay the costs of long-term care (LTC), if such care is needed. Regardless of whether you decide to buy LTC insurance, though, there are other coverages you must consider. For example, it is vital that you have insurance to help pay medical bills, which are bound to increase as you grow older.

First, the good news. When you reach age 65, you will qualify for Medicare, a federal health insurance program, regardless of your health. Thereafter, most medical bills will be covered. Medicare consists of two parts, A and B. Most participants pay nothing for Part A, which covers hospital bills; they pay a per month premium for Part B, which covers other medical expenses.

Now, the not-so-great tidings. Medicare does not cover everything. Patients, for example, are responsible for 20% of doctors' bills. On long hospital stays (over 60 days), patients must pay hundreds of dollars per day. Other exposures exist, including deductibles and co-payments; participants also may have to pay for checkups, immunizations, eyeglasses, and hearing aids. In 2006, partial coverage for drugs is available, under a new federal law. Those in traditional Medicare may enroll in a private plan that would have certain monthly costs, deductibles, and co-payments. The plan, in turn, would pay some of the costs of prescription drugs. Estimates indicate that enrolling in such a plan will pay off for those who will spend over $800 per year on prescriptions.

Moreover, such plans would pick up 95% of your drug costs, after you have spent a total of $3,600 per year. Thus, these plans will provide protection against catastrophic drug bills. (Seniors with low incomes would get subsidies so they will not face the costs involved with this drug coverage.)

- The Medicare+Choice program has been replaced by a Medicare Advantage program. Within Medicare Advantage, plans such as Medicare health maintenance organizations (HMOs) and Medicare preferred provider organizations (PPOs) will offer drug coverage in addition to other medical benefits.

- Some people with Medicare now receive prescription drug coverage through a former employer. The new law provides subsidies to encourage employers to maintain such coverage.

- Drug imports from Canada would remain banned, as under prior law. The new Medicare law also aims to speed the introduction of less-expensive generic drugs to the market by limiting the ability of pharmaceutical companies to create delays.

Choice Cuts

Concerns about drugs may affect the type of Medicare arrangement you choose. A few years ago, the federal government unveiled its Medicare+Choice program with great fanfare. In addition to traditional Medicare, participants could choose among HMOs, PPOs, medical savings accounts (MSAs), and various other options. The professed goal was to provide the elderly with cost-saving alternatives to traditional Medicare.

So far, though, Medicare alternatives have struggled. Few Medicare MSAs or Medicare PPOs have appeared. Medicare HMOs are available but the demand is hardly overwhelming. In fact, Medicare HMOs have dropped more than two million seniors since peaking in 1998. Some of those who were dropped have found other HMOs but the total number of enrollees has declined from 6 million to 5 million. (Overall, more than 40 million Americans are covered by Medicare, for a slight increase during this time period.)

Seniors who choose Medicare HMOs often have lower out-of-pocket costs and added benefits, including drug coverage, compared with those in traditional Medicare. As a tradeoff, Medicare HMO enrollees lack provider choice and must go through a gatekeeper system. In addition, there are no guarantees that an HMO will stay in the Medicare program from one year to the next; even if an HMO does stay in the Medicare program, there is no certainty the costs and services will remain the same. In each recent year, thousands of enrollees have lost coverage because their HMOs dropped out of Medicare; among the remaining Medicare HMOs, some have trimmed benefits and raised costs.

Enrolling in a Medicare HMO is often a less expensive choice. However, unless there is a financial problem, most seniors sign up for traditional Medicare and buy a supplemental insurance policy. Thus, the real "choice" in Medicare+Choice, for most seniors, is between the 10 standardized "Medigap policies," Plans A through J.

Medigap Plans, "A"Dequate To "J"Umbo

As the name suggests, Medigap insurance is designed to fill the gaps left by traditional Medicare. After reports that elderly buyers of health insurance were being abused, in 1990 Congress passed legislation creating 10 standard Medigap policies, labeled A through J. Each Plan must offer the same basic benefits, no more and no less.

Plan A covers what might be called basic exposure: hospital co-payments and doctor's bills up to Medicare-approved limits. As might be expected, the costs for Plan A are the lowest among Medigap policies. According to Weiss Ratings, a research firm in Jupiter, Florida, a 65-year-old female could pay as little as $355 a year for Plan A, in 2004. (It pays to shop around because insurers must offer Plan A if they want to offer any others in a particular state. Therefore, some companies may intentionally overprice Plan A, if they do not seek to sell that policy.)

Plan B is similar, except that it also covers the deductible for hospital stays. Beyond Plans A and B, a variety of additional features are available, such as coverage for skilled nursing care, foreign travel, excess doctors' bills, and even some (limited) reimbursements for prescription drugs. Such policies can be pricey: a fully-loaded Plan J (covering up to $3,000 worth of prescription drugs a year) may cost over $7,500 a year, for that 65-year-old female, according to Weiss Ratings. The company advises Medigap buyers that the cost of coverage can vary drastically by insurance provider, even for identical plans offering the same benefits in the same location.

Why are there such great disparities? In some cases, high premiums are caused by marketing strategies—companies do not want to sell a certain policy in a certain area, or they will sell it only at a very high price. Other differences include the way premiums change as consumers age, insurers' underwriting (selection) policies and their financial strength.

Should you shop for the least expensive Medigap coverage? A lower price certainly is an attractive feature but that is not all you should look for. You also want a company that keeps rates stable and pays claims promptly, so check with your insurance agent about a company's reputation before buying. Many life insurance agents also handle Medigap policies.

Filling The Gap

As mentioned, Medigap Plans H, I, and J include prescription drug benefits, with J offering the greatest coverage. These three plans no longer can be offered, as of 2006, when Medicare will begin covering some prescriptions, but existing policies may be maintained. Under the 2003 Medicare law, anyone who holds onto a Medigap policy with drug coverage will not be able to sign up for the new Medicare drug plan in 2006.

Veterans' Days

Seniors may receive drug coverage if they are veterans. As long as they have had at least six months of active military duty, they can get prescription drugs from the Veterans Administration for a modest (now $7) co-payment. However, many vets do not know about this program and wind up overpaying, perhaps for many years. If you are a vet, start the process at age 63 or 64 because it can take as long as 18 months to complete all the paperwork.

Another option, one that might appeal to non-veterans, is to cut drug costs as much as 60% by ordering them online, from Canada. The 2003 Medicare law forbids importation of Canadian drugs unless the Health and Human Services Department certifies their safety, which the department has refused to do. However, it may be impractical for the federal government to prosecute seniors for bringing in drugs from Canada while actions by states and cities may nullify the threat. Indeed, New Hampshire and Boston already have announced plans to bring in lower-cost Canadian drugs for some employees, retirees, Medicaid recipients, and prison inmates.

The Right Prescription

Those solutions will not work for everyone, though. Some seniors are not veterans and are not able to get the drugs they need from Canada. Sometimes, Medigap Plans H, I, and J are the only alternatives open.

Plans H, I, and J often are bought (if they are bought at all) by people who fully expect to have a high drug bill. When entering the Medicare Part B program (which covers doctors' bills), people are guaranteed access to Medigap policies, regardless of their health.

One strategy, then, is for people who anticipate substantial outlays for prescription drugs (or who want top-of-the-line policies) to sign up for Plans H, I, or J. Existing coverage can be retained, even if these plans are taken off the market in 2006.

Compared with Medigap policies, federal officials say that Medicare's drug coverage, which became available in 2006, will be a richer benefit. Under Medicare Part D, which is how the drug benefit will be known; beneficiaries will have lower costs for coinsurance as well as coverage for catastrophic drug costs. In addition, the federal drug benefit will provide Medicare enrollees with significant discounts from retail prices.

While it is true that the new Medicare drug benefit may be better than anything offered under Medigap now, it remains to be seen how much the new Medicare drug coverage will cost. It has been estimated that Medicare's drug plan will cost $35 a month. However, insurers now charge around $100 per month to add drug coverage under Medigap Plan J, which is not as generous as what Medicare will offer.

How will insurance companies be able to offer more of a benefit for less money? When all the numbers are crunched, Medicare Part D may wind up charging so much that it will be out of reach for many seniors. Medicare Part D is to come from private insurers, and it will be up to them to determine how much to charge consumers who sign up for this voluntary benefit.

Signing up for (or keeping) Medigap Plans H, I, or J now gives you the option of holding onto that coverage, if Medigap Part D proves to be disappointing, or switching into Part D if that seems to be a wise move, in 2006. At that point, seniors who sign up for Medicare Part D can convert a Medigap Plan H-I-J to another Medigap plan.

That's Life

Seniors certainly will need health insurance, whether it is obtained via a Medicare-Medigap combination or through a Medicare HMO. The case for buying or keeping life insurance, though, is not so clear-cut: there may be a time when your life insurance can be reduced or dropped altogether.

The most basic need for life insurance comes when you are the main breadwinner in a family with pre-school and school-age children. In case of your untimely death, your income will be sorely missed. The purchase of life insurance can protect your family by filling the financial gap.

More decisions have to be made as your children finish their education and begin to live independently. At this point, your death probably will not be as financially devastating as it would have been 10 or 20 years earlier. Not only have your responsibilities declined, you may well have accumulated other assets, such as an investment portfolio, a retirement fund, and equity in your home. Moreover, the cost of buying life insurance might have increased significantly with your age.

For seniors, the decision about dropping or reducing life insurance will not be simple. How much security do you want to provide for your surviving spouse, who might live for decades after you are gone? Maybe you will want to provide a few years of financial security, during which period your spouse can make a transition to a more modest lifestyle.

There may be other reasons you will want, if not exactly need, life insurance: a desire to provide an inheritance for your children or to make a substantial bequest to a favorite cause. These are all value judgments, with no "right" answers, but they need to be considered thoughtfully.

Type-Casting

After you decide how much (if any) life insurance is needed, you must choose which type of insurance to buy. Life insurance falls into two broad categories:

Term insurance. This is pure insurance, covering you for a specified time period. As you grow older and your life expectancy decreases, the cost of term insurance increases. However, price competition has been holding down the cost of term coverage and the recent proliferation of insurance Web sites on the Internet has heightened this competition.

Permanent insurance. These policies are much more expensive than term insurance but the excess amounts you pay go into an investment account, sometimes called the "cash value." Eventually the cash value may be tapped by policyholders or used to pay for the policy premiums as you grow older. Various types of permanent insurance are known as "whole life," "universal life," and "variable life" insurance.

Which category makes the most sense? Term insurance is much less expensive but permanent life insurance deserves some consideration. In many cases, the need for life insurance remains in place much longer than you expect. Whenever you keep an insurance policy for more than 10 years, there is a strong case for permanent insurance.

The appeal of permanent life insurance is driven largely by tax advantages. Inside an insurance policy the buildup of cash value will not be subject to income tax. What's more, tax-free withdrawals and loans are permitted, up to certain limits. (For both term and permanent insurance, death benefits usually are free of income tax.) Long-term, the payoff to you and your family may be worth paying the extra premiums.

Today, among permanent insurance policies, most people prefer universal life and variable universal life. With universal life, you have flexibility regarding how much you pay in premiums. Any excess, above the cost of pure term insurance, earns a return that is comparable to bond yields.

Variable universal life (VUL) offers the same premium flexibility. However, the excess premiums can be allocated among several investment accounts, many of which resemble mutual funds. Indeed, top mutual fund managers may call the shots for these "subaccounts." The payoff, then, is that your cash value may rise in step with the stock market, providing more insurance protection over the long term. (Your account value may fall with the stock market, too.)

The ability to choose your investments has been driving demand for VUL. Long-term, it is very likely that the equity subaccounts will outperform policies offering a fixed return. The earlier you get started, the better: not only will you be getting more value, in paying for life insurance, you will have a longer time for the equity accounts to grow.

Cash Cows

Permanent life insurance policies may be divided in another manner: those emphasizing a large death benefit, in relation to the premiums paid, and those featuring cash accumulation. Premiums are relatively higher, for the latter type, but many seniors plan to take tax-free policy loans and withdrawals to provide supplementary retirement income.

The problem with such strategies, however, is that arranging for policy loans and withdrawals can be an arduous process. Not every insurer allows your money to be transferred from an insurance policy to another account automatically, on a regular schedule. Seniors also must avoid taking too much from the policy, which would force the policy to lapse and trigger back taxes.

If you are interested in a cash accumulation policy, ask the company if such an automatic transfer program is in place. If so, you may eventually enjoy years of tax-free cash flow in retirement, along with the peace of mind of knowing that the cash will flow to your loved ones, even if you never make it to your own golden years.

Liquid Assets

For many seniors, though, life insurance is neither a family protection vehicle nor a supplemental retirement plan. Instead, life insurance proceeds can be counted on to provide liquidity when it is needed. With proper planning, insurance money can pay an estate tax bill and leave other assets intact.

Suppose, for example, that Joan Brown dies and leaves a large estate to her son Adam. Substantial estate tax is due. However, most of Joan's assets are tied up in real estate, shares of a family business, and an IRA.

Adam does not want to sell the family company or the real estate. If he taps the inherited IRA to raise cash, he will have to pay income tax on the withdrawal and lose a valuable opportunity for extended tax deferral.

Anticipating such a problem, Joan buys insurance on her own life. The proceeds can be used to pay the estate tax bill. Thanks to the liquidity provided by life insurance, Adam can hold onto the real estate and the family business while taking only minimum required distributions from the inherited IRA.

What's more, as long as the insurance policy is owned by Adam or by a trust, the proceeds probably will not be included in Joan's estate and will not increase the estate tax obligation. If you are interested in such a strategy, you should buy permanent rather than term insurance. You will want a policy that remains in place, no matter when you die.

Policy Payoffs

Even if estate tax liquidity is not an issue, you might want to include life insurance in your estate plan, for various reasons:

Buy-sell agreements. If you are a business owner or part-owner, such an agreement is a must, to protect yourself and your loved ones. Buy-sells often rely upon life insurance to provide the necessary funding.

Extra cash. If you are leaving real estate or a family business to one child, life insurance proceeds can provide the cash to compensate other children, evening out the inheritance.

Family protection. In case there is an anticipated need, life insurance can provide greater financial security to your survivors, after your death.

Long-term care replenishment. Life insurance might be considered an alternative to LTC insurance. If you do wind up having to spend substantial sums for custodial care, life insurance proceeds can provide extra cash for the beneficiaries, replacing the wealth lost to LTC expenses.

Charitable bequests. Life insurance may be used to provide for charity at your death, without depriving your heirs.

Switch Hit

For the above purposes, you may want life insurance that will not expire. However, permanent insurance can be expensive. Instead, you might want to buy convertible term coverage for such concerns. Term insurance is relatively inexpensive now and these policies can be converted to permanent insurance if you discover a need (such as estate tax liquidity) you will not outlive. If you already have permanent insurance and decide you no longer need the coverage, read the fine print before cashing in. Many policies have severe surrender charges in place for 10 years or longer.

Even if surrender charges are not an issue, bailing out of a permanent life insurance policy may trigger income taxes. Instead, you can enter into a "1035 exchange," tax-free, for a low-cost annuity. Subsequently, you can stop paying the premiums or pay a smaller amount. The new contract eventually might be annuitized, providing a partially tax-sheltered stream of income.

Second Best

Married couples might prefer "second-to-die" or "survivorship" life insurance for estate planning purposes. Such policies insure the lives of both spouses, then pay off only after the second death. Because the payment will be delayed, survivorship policies tend to be much less expensive than policies covering one life. Under the tax code, spousal bequests are excluded from estate tax. Therefore, estate taxes might not be due until the death of the second spouse. At that time, a survivorship policy can provide the needed liquidity.

Suppose, for example, Jim Walker dies in 2006 with a $10 million estate. He leaves $2 million to his children, the amount that can be passed on, tax-free. The other $8 million can be left to his wife Linda—the unlimited marital deduction provides shelter so Jim's estate owes no tax. At Linda's death, though, estate tax probably will be due, depending on how much is left and the then-current tax law. To guard against this possibility, the Walkers have purchased a $4 million survivorship policy, which is held in trust. When Linda dies, this policy will pay $4 million, which can be used to pay $4 million worth of estate tax and other expenses. This liquidity may permit the parents' estate to pass largely intact to their children.

(For more on sophisticated estate planning strategies, see Chapter 4.)

8

Investment Planning

◆

Silver Heads and Golden Needings

In this era of scarce pensions and uncertain Social Security, it is vital for seniors to be able to finance their own lifestyle. In essence, it is up to you to save and invest for a comfortable retirement. Just a few years ago, investing for the future seemed easy. All you had to do was load up on tech stocks and watch them grow by 20% a year—or even faster. The subsequent stock market collapse of 2000–2002 not only ravaged many retirement funds, it also reminded investors of the importance of asset allocation. That is, you should hold a diversified mix of stocks, bonds, cash, and perhaps other types of assets in your portfolio. Investment professionals generally agree that asset allocation is the most important factor affecting long-term investment returns. Stock-picking and market timing are much less influential in determining how much you will accumulate from your investments.

What's more, asset allocation can reduce the risk of investing. Anyone who held only dot-com stocks suffered tremendous losses during the recent bear market. On the other hand, investors who held some tech stocks, some bank stocks, some real estate securities, some bonds, etc., held their own or wound up with overall gains during that period.

Older, Not Bolder

If you would rather not master the intricacies of asset allocation, some mutual fund companies will do it for you. Fidelity, Vanguard, and T. Rowe Price, for example, have funds that target specific dates when investors expect to retire. There might be a 2010 fund, a 2015 fund, etc. These funds become more conservative as retirement approaches and such an allocation becomes more appropriate. Typically, as your retirement draws near, assets will be shifted from stock funds to bond funds and cash, within these "target maturity" funds. Eventually, you will wind up in a retirement income fund. Target maturity funds are not all alike, though. Some are more aggressive than others, meaning that they hold more equities, deeper into an individual's life. The end-of-the-line retirement income funds, though, will have fewer stocks and more bonds or cash reserves.

Location, Location

The old saying holds that the three most important factors to consider when investing in real estate are "location, location, and location." When investing for retirement, two "locations" will do: you must decide which assets should be held inside a tax-deferred retirement plan and which should be held on the outside, in a taxable account.

Many advisors suggest holding high-income assets inside of a tax-deferred account, where the tax on that income can be deferred. Ideally, investment income not taxed this year, at rates up to 35%, will be taxed years in the future, perhaps when a retiree is in the 25% tax bracket.

In essence, this approach means holding bonds inside a retirement plan, where tax on the interest can be deferred, while stocks are held on the outside. Unrealized stock market appreciation remains untaxed, perhaps forever, and realized gains may be taxed at favorable rates.

This will not be an issue if you do all of your investing inside a tax-deferred retirement plan. Say you have a $500,000 IRA and you favor a 60-40 allocation, stocks to bonds. You would hold $300,000 in stocks in your IRA, along with $200,000 in bonds.

The situation is different, though, if you have $250,000 in your IRA and $250,000 in a taxable account. If so, you have to decide which assets go where. Several factors might affect your asset location decision:

The 2000–2002 bear market. The possibility of taking more losses in equities makes it more appealing to hold stocks outside of a retirement plan. Net capital losses provide tax breaks on the outside but no advantages inside a retirement account.

Also, investors' expectations for stock market returns have been lowered by recent events. The greater the expected return from stocks, the more sense it makes to defer the tax on those gains, and vice versa.

Low interest rates. While yields are very low for Treasury bonds and top-rated municipals, corporate bonds may make sense. Corporate bonds are fully taxable so they work best inside a retirement plan.

Taxable bonds generally yield more than tax-exempt bonds of the same maturity and credit quality. Therefore, you can pick up extra yield with the same amount of risk by buying taxable bonds in your IRA, rather than buying tax-exempt bonds outside.

Low tax rates on dividends. Now that dividends are taxed at only 15%, dividend-paying stocks may work best outside of a retirement plan. Inside of a plan, this tax break is wasted. In fact, holding dividend-paying stocks inside a tax-deferred retirement plan means converting tax-favored income to fully-taxable income, upon withdrawal.

Loss Leaders

The basic strategy, then, is to hold stocks and stock funds outside of your retirement plan. If so, you can take capital losses when they occur. Realized losses may either be deducted, over time, or used to offset future gains. While you take losses on stocks that fall, you can let your winners ride, largely untaxed. Long-term gains likely will enjoy favorable tax rates; currently, that rate can be as low as 5%.

In fact, long-term capital gains might not be taxed at all. That may be true for stocks passed on to heirs or donated to charity.

While holding stocks outside of a retirement plan, you can keep taxable bonds—probably corporate bonds and bond funds—inside your plan. The taxes on the interest can be deferred until money is withdrawn.

Know Where To Hold 'Em

Such a stocks-out, bonds-in strategy might work well if your holdings exactly match your asset allocation. Say you have $300,000 in a taxable account and $200,000 in your IRA. Your basic asset allocation is 60-40, stocks to bonds. In such a situation, your stocks stay out while your bonds go in.

Most portfolios, though, do not line up so neatly. Often, either your stock or your bond allocation will exceed the size of the desired account so some spillover is likely.

If your IRA is relatively small, some of your bonds may have to be held in a taxable account. You probably will want to hold tax-exempt municipal bonds or Treasuries, which pay interest that is not subject to state or local income tax.

On the other hand, if your IRA is relatively large, some of your equities may have to be held in there. In this case, you will have to decide *which* stocks or stock funds go inside. Certain equities should be the first ones to go inside your IRA:

Real estate investment trusts (REITs) and REIT funds. REITs pay high dividends, which can be sheltered from current taxation, inside a retirement account. Some of the dividends paid by REITs are not taxable but most of the yield to investors is taxable, at your highest tax rate, so they belong inside a retirement plan.

Small-company stocks. Often, promising small-capitalization stocks are difficult to identify so many investors invest in this asset class through mutual funds. Small-cap mutual funds, especially index funds, frequently recognize gains. Successful small-caps become mid-caps, which may force funds to sell them, taking profits. Such gains, which may be short-term gains, can be sheltered from current taxation inside of a tax-deferred retirement plan.

Hybrid funds that buy some bonds to go with their stocks are better held inside an IRA.

What's more, all types of high-turnover funds that are doing well at the time of investment can go inside your IRA because they will have to pay out their gains, producing a tax bill. Likewise, as year-end approaches you may want to put mutual funds you buy inside an IRA if you think the funds may pay a sizable dividend.

Hedge funds. Technically, hedge funds are considered an alternative asset class, rather than equities or fixed-income. However, they resemble stocks because they are risky and have the potential for high returns. Hedge funds are tax-inefficient if held on the outside because they may generate short-term gains without cash distributions. Thus, if you invest in hedge funds, this asset class may be held inside a tax-deferred account, if that is feasible. Other vehicles that work like hedge funds, such as managed futures funds, also may work well inside a retirement plan. Generally, if you must hold equities or equity-like instruments inside of a tax-deferred retirement plan, choose the investments that are likely to generate the highest tax bill, year after year.

On the other hand, large-company domestic stocks and funds holding such stocks should be held outside a retirement plan, if possible. Especially if you invest through index funds, and you tend to hold for the long term, such stocks and funds can be very tax-efficient so there is little to be gained by holding them inside a retirement account.

On Target

Building a retirement fund may be vital because the date you retire might depend upon your investment success. Often, retirement age is the date when someone has accumulated enough wealth to support him or herself comfortably, without earned income. While retirement planning may have become more elegant, thanks to powerful software, two numbers remain crucial for answering the "How much is enough?" question. First, how much will you want to spend after you retire; second, how large an investment portfolio have you accumulated? The ratio of these two numbers generally will determine whether retirement is feasible.

The maximum draw with which many advisors feel comfortable, assuming that a retiree is young and in good health, is 4%. From there, you back into a retirement goal. Someone retiring at age 70 can be a little more aggressive with the draw, because of the shorter retirement period, so you might go up to 6.5% or 7%. That is, if you retire at age 65 with a $1 million portfolio, you could comfortably withdraw $40,000, assuming a 4% withdrawal rate, while a much older retiree might withdraw as much as 7%. (Retirement projections usually assume that these initial amounts increase each year, to keep up with inflation.)

Turning these numbers around, in order to retire comfortably, you must accumulate 15 to 25 times the amount you wish to spend in retirement, if you want to avoid running short of money. If you assume a retirement in the 60–65 age range, living until the late 90s, and spending $125,000 to $150,000 per year, after-tax, and there is no pension, you would probably need $2.5 million to $3 million. The amount needed would be at the upper end of that range, if the portfolio is mainly held in an IRA, because withdrawals probably would be taxable.

Not everyone will want to spend $125,000+ in retirement but many people will want to spend $40,000, $80,000, or more each year. What if you cannot accumulate a portfolio of $1 million, $2 million or more? Can you ever afford to retire? Yes, but concessions may be necessary. One option that may be practical for many people is to keep working. Each year you continue to work can help you reach your retirement goals. It is another year in which you can fund your retirement portfolio while you are not consuming assets. If you continue to work, the multiple of spending will go down, when calculating how much is enough. That is, if you want to spend $50,000 per year in retirement, it is easier to accumulate $750,000 (15 times $50,000) than $1.25 million (25 times $50,000), which could mean waiting until age 70 to retire, rather than age 60.

On The House

Another possible approach is to liquidate non-financial assets to provide additional capital. The continued strength of the housing market may mean that real estate will play a large role in some seniors' retirement plans. If you own two homes, for example, selling one of those homes will help provide money for retirement.

Seniors owning one home also may find retirement funds there. You can downsize a personal residence and even move to another area of the country where housing is less expensive. The tax code helps because you can sell a house and exclude some capital gains from your taxable income. This tax break, which applies to a primary residence after two years' occupancy, permits a $250,000 exclusion for single taxpayers and $500,000 for married couples.

Not everyone is willing or able to keep working or cash in home equity. Many people, though, can increase the pace of pre-retirement investing to build a larger retirement fund. Yet another strategy is to spend less in retirement. Even if near-retirement projections show that your goals will not be met in full, you need not despair.

Someone might have $800,000 in a retirement plan and $500,000 in other money. Assuming a 5% withdrawal rate, this hypothetical $1.3 million retirement fund would produce $65,000 a year, pre-tax, which might not be what you would like for your retirement. Still, you can afford to retire, even if you will not have the retirement you had hoped for.

As mentioned, returning to work may be another fallback option for some seniors facing retirement. In addition to such post-"retirement" earnings, other sources of income should be recognized while seeking the how-much number.

A couple might have a goal of $70,000 worth of retirement income, for example. If that couple has $20,000 coming from Social Security benefits, they only need $50,000 from their investment portfolio, and $50,000 per year from a portfolio is a much more manageable number than $70,000.

With competent planning, a senior can enjoy a rewarding retirement with an even smaller portfolio. Some people retire with $100,000 in investment assets; they live conservatively and they are very comfortable. The more you can accumulate while you are still working, though, the more comfortable your retirement can be.

Lack of Interest

When you are building a retirement fund, you probably would want to hold a fair amount of equities. Long-term, stocks probably will deliver superior returns. Once you retire, though, the picture changes. Chances are that you will want to hold onto some equities, for growth potential, but your focus is likely to shift to bonds and other fixed-income vehicles, which can provide income once you stop working. In addition, a bond-heavy portfolio will not be badly clawed in the next bear market. The catch, though, is that yields on bank accounts, bonds, etc., are depressingly low in the early years of the 21st century. In this environment, where are seniors likely to find decent yields?

Bond ladders. With a bond ladder, maturities are staggered so that bonds mature periodically. As bonds mature, redemption proceeds are re-invested at the far-out ladder rung. This technique allows frequent reinvestment, to hedge against rising interest rates, while you assemble a portfolio of bonds bought at longer maturities, to lock in decent yields against future declines. You might, for example, build a ladder of bonds maturing at yearly intervals, going out as far as 10 years. You will pick up a great deal of additional income without adding a huge amount of volatility.

Investment-grade, but lower-grade. Whether or not you ladder your fixed-income holdings, you can earn extra yields by investing in corporate bonds rather than Treasuries. That is, you can pick up some extra yield by going down in credit quality but staying in the lower level of investment-grade rather than going into junk bonds. Such bonds might yield one point more than Treasuries of the same maturity.

Callable bonds. In corporates, buying callable bonds (bonds that can be redeemed prior to the stated maturity date) is another strategy for squeezing out perhaps 0.5% of extra yield. In return for more yields, you must accept these tradeoffs:

- Reinvestment risk. Bonds usually are called if interest rates have dropped. If so, investors who want to reinvest will receive lower yields.

- Price compression. Investors holding callable bonds can lose, if interest rates rise, but they cannot gain very much if rates drop because the bonds might be redeemed at par or slightly higher.

Long-term municipals. High-income seniors might prefer municipal bonds and muni bond funds, which offer tax-exempt yields, to corporate bonds and funds. Some munis offer excellent value these days, with yields that may be almost as high as Treasury yields. After-tax, high-bracket investors will wind up better off with munis.

Among munis, the highest yields are paid by long-term bonds. Long-, medium-, or short-term, insured municipal bonds appeal to investors seeking an extra layer of credit risk.

Foreign bonds. The search for yield can be literally world-wide these days, as investors consider bonds issued outside the U.S. With foreign bonds, currency risk dwarfs other factors such as credit or interest-rate risk. The U.S. dollar is generally expected to weaken in the coming years, which adds to the appeal of bonds issued in other currencies.

Foreign bonds are not only a bet against the dollar; they also can help to diversify a fixed-income portfolio. They have a lower correlation to stocks than U.S. corporate bonds and they're less sensitive to interest rate movements. Foreign bond funds have modest yields, though; funds that hold bonds from emerging markets may offer yields that are nearly twice as high. Emerging markets bonds may do well if there is a world-wide economic recovery, which now seems possible. Rising commodity prices will help some of those countries.

Dividend-paying stocks. Under the 2003 tax law, most investors will pay only 15% tax on dividends while those in low tax brackets (which might include retirees) will pay a mere 5% tax on dividends. Many stocks with long histories of increasing dividends also have posted substantial growth, over the years.

Keep the Cash Flowing

Unfortunately, in this era of low-yield bonds and low-dividend stocks, it is difficult if not impossible to live comfortably from investment income. Instead, it is likely that your retirement fund must be tapped regularly, to support a comfortable lifestyle. However, if you withdraw too much from this fund, too soon, you or your spouse might run low on spending money, during a lengthy retirement.

Keeping those concerns in mind, how much can you prudently withdraw from your retirement fund each year? You might start with a reasonable amount in the first year of retirement. Then increase your withdrawal each year to keep pace with inflation. Although some advisors favor a 4% initial draw, 5% may be considered a sensible initial withdrawal rate. If you have a $1 million portfolio, you might withdraw $50,000 the first full year of retirement. If inflation is then 3%, you would increase your withdrawal by 3%, to $51,500. And so on, year after year. This procedure maintains your purchasing power because your retirement income will keep up with inflation.

The question then, is *where* $50,000 will come from in Year One, $51,500 in Year Two, etc. Should those withdrawals come from a tax-deferred plan, such as an IRA, or from money held in a taxable account? Often, drawing down the taxable account first makes sense. Keeping money in your IRA permits a longer period of tax deferral, which generally works to your advantage. Moreover, withdrawing money from your IRA before age 59-1/2 usually leads to a 10% penalty tax so you probably should avoid IRA withdrawals before then, if possible. If you must tap your IRA before 59-1/2, some exceptions to this penalty apply. The process is complicated so you will probably need professional advice to develop a penalty-free withdrawal plan, before age 59-1/2.

Avoiding Withdrawal Pains

The situation changes after you reach age 70-1/2, though. You must take minimum required distributions (MRD) from your IRA or pay a 50% penalty for any shortfall. Again, calculating MRDs is not easy so you should work with a knowledgeable advisor. Once you are at the MRD stage, you should plan your withdrawals around your required distributions. Suppose, for example, at age 75 you want to withdraw $55,000 from your retirement funds while your MRD that year turns out to be $40,000. If so, you might take $40,000 from your IRA, as required, and the other $15,000 from a taxable account. Be aware, though, that money coming from your IRA will be reduced by income tax and adjust your spending plans accordingly.

Reap What You Have Sown

Beyond the question of which pocket to pick, retirees need to decide which assets to liquidate, assuming that interest and dividends will not provide the necessary $50,000, $60,000, or whatever is needed for retirement spending. To make such decisions easier, you probably should keep 12–18 months' of spending money in a cash reserve such as a money market fund.

Say you want to spend $80,000 over the next 12 months, in addition to what you will get from Social Security. Thus, you should keep $80,000-$120,000 in a money market fund, for ready access. As the need arises, money can be transferred from this cash reserve to a checking account, to pay bills. Alternatively, you can arrange for regular transfers, simulating a "paycheck" coming into your checking account from your money market fund. Having an ample sum in a money market fund will enable you to meet emergencies if they arise. You will not have to make hurried portfolio decisions during times of stress.

Fixed For Life

Beyond stocks and bonds and cash, investing for retirement might involve annuities. For seniors, annuities can offer advantages but you should know the basic terminology before you invest.

One option is a *deferred fixed annuity*, usually known as a fixed annuity. Fixed annuities can provide bond-like yields, protection against interest-rate fluctuations, and deferral of income tax. You can buy a fixed annuity from an insurance company or another financial firm, with a single premium or with a series of premiums.

In most cases, you will receive a set yield for a set period of time. You might, for example, get 3% per year on a three-year contract or 4% on a five-year commitment. When the initial term is up, the yield will be re-set. As long as your annuity is in the accumulation stage, and you make no withdrawals, no income tax will be due. With a fixed annuity, there are no minimum required distributions, as there are with IRAs and other retirement plans.

What if the annuity issuer offers, say, 3% on a three-year contract then drops the yield when it is re-set? You can exchange your unappealing annuity for another one, tax-free.

You need to be aware that fixed annuities may have surrender charges in place for several years. However, if you change into a so-called "bonus" annuity, an upfront payment might offset any surrender charge you incur.

Forever Funds

Eventually, you may "annuitize" your fixed annuity, converting the contract value to a stream of cash flow. If so, you might receive an income that is guaranteed for your life, no matter how long you live. Another option is to receive a lower monthly payment that will last as long as either you or your spouse is alive.

If you annuitize your contract, you will receive cash flow that is partly tax-sheltered. Say you invest $80,000 in a fixed annuity. Eventually, the contract value grows to $200,000. You annuitize over your own life expectancy, at an age when you are receiving $1,600 per month, or $19,200 per year. (The older you are when you annuitize, the higher the monthly payments.)

In this example ($80,000 grows to $200,000), 40% of each payment is considered a tax-free return of your investment. Thus, if you receive $19,200 per year in annuity payments, only 60% ($11,520) will be taxable income. If you live past your life expectancy and collect annuity payments after receiving your $80,000 return-of-principal, subsequent payments will be fully taxable.

Better Than Bonds?

Fixed annuities can provide valuable tax deferral. However, the tax disadvantages should not be overlooked. If you tap your contract before you annuitize, withdrawals will be fully taxable until you have pulled out all of your earnings. In addition, withdrawals from fixed annuities are subject to a 10% penalty before age 59-1/2. Thus, if you invest in a fixed annuity, you should be prepared to hold on until at least age 59-1/2, before you begin withdrawals. Given these pros and cons, are fixed annuities better than bonds or bond funds? Perhaps, especially when interest rates are expected to rise.

Most fixed annuities are not devalued when rates rise. Contract values do not decline. Instead, fixed annuities may actually perform well in times of rising rates. When your years of receiving 3% end, the yield on your fixed annuity might be reset at 4% or 5%.

Not only can fixed annuities offer advantages over bonds, they can appeal to stock market investors, too. In recent years, the fastest-growing type of fixed annuity has been the equity-index annuity (EIA). These are linked to a stock market index, such as the S&P 500. Investors get a guaranteed return, tax-deferred, as they would from a traditional fixed annuity, but that return might go even higher if the relevant stock index performs well. Although EIAs will not give you all of the return you might get from the stock market, they generally offer a minimum guarantee that you will not get from stocks.

Stock Answers

For more exposure to the stock market, along with more risk, you might consider a *deferred variable annuity*, usually referred to as a variable annuity. Compared with fixed annuities, variable annuities provide a return that depends on the success of the investment accounts within the annuity contract.

Variable annuities typically offer a menu of investment accounts that includes several stock funds and bond funds. Many investors choose to invest largely in stock funds because the potential returns may be greater than a fixed annuity will provide.

Suppose, for example, Jim Davis invests $100,000 in a variable annuity. Jim might allocate his investment among a large-cap growth account, a large-cap value account, a small-company account, a real estate stock account, and an international stock account. While he holds his variable annuity, Jim can move money among these various accounts and add new investment choices, if they seem appealing. No income tax will be due until money is withdrawn.

The greater the contract value, the greater the cash flow that will be paid, if Jim decides to annuitize his variable annuity. Suppose, for example, Jim decides to annuitize his variable annuity at age 72, when his wife Nancy is 70. If Jim has $250,000 in his contract then, he and Nancy might receive around $1,500 per month ($18,000 a year), as long as either is alive. However, if the annuity contract is worth only $125,000 then, they might receive $750 per month, or $9,000 a year.

Upside, No Downside

As you can see, there is no way of knowing that Jim's equity accounts will grow from $100,000 to $250,000, or even to $125,000. As the 2000–2002 bear market has revealed, equity markets may fall and Jim's contract value may drop below $100,000.

Traditionally, variable annuities have offered guaranteed death benefits. Suppose, in our example, Jim dies at age 70, before he annuitizes his contract. If the value of the contract is $250,000, Jim's beneficiary Nancy would receive that amount. However, suppose the contract value is only $80,000 when Jim dies. A traditional variable annuity would pay Nancy the $100,000 that Jim invested. Thus, Jim's beneficiary is protected from any investment losses inside the variable annuity.

In recent years, some variable annuities have added further guarantees. The guaranteed value might be stepped up at an anniversary date or it might automatically increase each year. With these enhanced guarantees, Nancy might receive an amount greater than $100,000, in the above example. Therefore, variable annuities have provided guarantees to an investor's beneficiary. In recent years, so-called living benefits have been added to most variable annuities. With living benefits, the investor himself or herself receives the guarantee. Thus, a substantial stream of retirement income can be assured, for the investor and perhaps for a surviving spouse as well. Such guarantees may provide comfort to cautious investors, enabling them to invest in potentially rewarding equity accounts without worrying that the stock market will turn down.

Immediate Gratification

As opposed to the deferred annuities described above, an *immediate annuity* (which may now be called a "payout annuity" or an "income annuity) starts paying out right away. Typically, these annuities promises to provide you (and perhaps your spouse as well) with lifetime income.

According to Ibbotson Associates, Chicago, a leading research firm, the probability of a favorable outcome is increased if investors' portfolios are divided between annuitized assets and non-annuitized assets. Even with supposedly safe withdrawal rates from an investment portfolio, investors may still run short of money. If you overlay annuities, for part of the portfolio, your prospects look much better.

Instead of relying, say, upon a $1 million investment portfolio, you might put $250,000 into an immediate annuity, thus guaranteeing a lifelong stream of income. The other $750,000 could remain invested; with the annuity in place, providing life-long income, your portfolio might tilt towards equities, for growth potential and inflation protection.

A few years ago, when stock market returns of over 20% per year were taken for granted, the yields offered by immediate annuities (around 4%-5%, as of this writing) seemed meager. Now, though, seniors may be willing to trade some stock market uncertainty for the peace of mind of guaranteed income. Again, immediate annuities offer not only the security of lifelong income but also tax benefits. Each payment is partially untaxed as a return of principal, at least initially. Generally, the tax-free treatment ends after you have received the amount you invested in the contract.

Flex Plans

Balancing out these advantages are some drawbacks to immediate annuities, but they may be overcome. You do not have to take a fixed amount and lock yourself into a loss of purchasing power. Many insurers offer immediate annuities with cost-of-living increases, to provide inflation protection. The initial payment will be relatively low, though.

Another alternative is to buy an immediate variable annuity, which can provide long-term growth, if the investment accounts do well. Some immediate variable annuities come with a floor for downside protection.

For example, a 65-year-old couple might get $650 per month, as long as either lives, from a $100,000 joint-and-survivor fixed immediate annuity. A variable immediate annuity might pay only $360 per month, upfront, yet have the potential to double in a five-year bull market. An 80% floor ($288 per month, in this example) would provide some bear market protection for seniors willing to take such risks.

Nevertheless, seniors may be wary of the loss of liquidity most immediate annuities require. Some people might not want to give up $100,000 today, as seen on an account statement, in return for a stream of $650 checks. An event might occur that would require a substantial amount of cash, such as the need to spend heavily on long-term care.

Increasingly, there may be solutions to this perceived problem. Some insurers provide a liquidity option: they might put a value on the expected remaining income stream and allow you access to that capital. However, there may be only certain time periods when you can do this, so you cannot go right from the doctor's office after hearing bad news to cash in your immediate annuity, and there might be some sort of medical report required.

Considering the pros and cons, you probably should not put more than one-third of your portfolio into an immediate annuity. If you are interested in this vehicle, an immediate annuity probably should be held outside of a retirement plan, so other assets can stay inside, where the taxes will be deferred.

9

Defer and Conquer

◆

How to Handle Your IRA After You Retire

Chances are you are saving for retirement in a tax-deferred, employer-sponsored plan such as a 401(k), Keogh, or profit-sharing plan. When you retire or change jobs, you will have to decide what to do with that account. The first choice, for many people, is to rollover the balance to an IRA. This strategy maintains the tax deferral while you control how your money will be invested. However, an IRA rollover is not your only choice. Instead, you can choose among the following alternatives:

Take the cash from your account. This will put spending money in your pocket right away. Any cash you get, though, will be taxable income. You also may owe a 10% early withdrawal penalty if you withdraw cash before age 59-1/2.

Keep the money in your former employer's plan. Many plans permit employees who leave to keep their money in place.

Transfer money to a new employer's plan. If you are moving to a new job, the plan there likely will accept rollovers, so the tax deferral can continue. In some cases, there will be a waiting period before you can contribute to the new plan. Even if you are not yet eligible to participate, you can hold cash in the new plan until you can make other investments.

Split the account. You can withdraw some of your retirement funds, pay tax (and perhaps a penalty) on the withdrawal, and roll the balance into a tax-deferred IRA.

Alternative Routes

As mentioned, an IRA rollover might be considered the default option. Nevertheless, there are times when you might choose one of the alternatives listed above. For example, the creditor protection of IRAs is subject to state law, in many situations, and not all states extend full protection to IRAs. In contrast, money held inside an employer-sponsored plan enjoys creditor protection under federal law. In addition, up to $1 million in IRAs and Roth IRAs is protected from creditors under Federal law. Therefore, you should check your state law before executing an IRA rollover, if creditor protection is important to you.

A local attorney can advise on the law in your state. This may not be an issue, if your state fully protects IRAs. In states where IRA protection is weak, though, you may prefer to keep your money in your former employer's plan or roll to a new employer's plan, if either of those options is available, in order to enjoy protection from creditors, judgments, divorce settlements, etc.

There may be a problem, though, with keeping your money inside an employer's plan. If you die with money inside an employer's plan, and someone other than your spouse is the beneficiary, some long-term tax deferral might be lost. In this situation, then, you may have to choose between creditor protection and the opportunity to provide a child or grandchild with years of valuable tax-deferred compounding.

Beyond creditor protection, there might be other reasons for choosing against a rollover. If you need to spend some or all of the money in your plan, you might as well withdraw it right away. That is especially true if you were born before 1936. People in that age group qualify for a special tax break, 10-year averaging, if they take all of their money out of a plan. With 10-year averaging, you may owe tax at a relatively low rate but this tax break is lost forever after an IRA rollover. Even if you cannot use 10-year averaging, today's low tax rates may make withdrawals appealing.

Another reason for passing up an IRA rollover might be a reluctance to spend time managing your own retirement fund or to spend money hiring a professional advisor. In that situation, you may prefer to leave the money with a former employer's plan or transfer it to a new one. Inside an employer's plan, professionals handle the investment decisions. Moreover, the plan sponsor (the employer) has a fiduciary responsibility to manage money for growth as well as for capital preservation. If you have your retirement fund in a plan sponsored by a large organization, you may take comfort from the fact that a substantial entity has this obligation to provide for your retirement.

Work Zone

Another situation could arise if you go into semi-retirement, perhaps working part-time. If you roll the money into an IRA, you must start taking distributions (and paying income tax) after you reach 70-1/2. In a company plan, tax deferral can continue. You must still be working and you cannot own more than 5% of the company. Therefore, keeping your money in an employer's plan may enable you to extend tax deferral until you completely stop working.

Many employer-sponsored plans offer another advantage: they permit you to borrow half your account balance, up to $50,000. Such loans may be easier to get than bank loans, with less paperwork. Also, repayments (plus interest) go to your retirement account rather than to a bank. You cannot borrow from an IRA. In fact, any outstanding loans must be repaid before a rollover, reducing the amount you will have in your IRA. Therefore, if you have outstanding loans, or think you might want to borrow in the future, keeping money in an employer's plan may be the best choice.

Penalty Box

Early retirees may face yet another judgment call. As mentioned, withdrawing money from an IRA before age 59-1/2 may expose you to a 10% penalty. Thus, if you need to tap your retirement funds, you might not want to enter into a roll-over before that age. Under the tax code, you can take money from an employer-sponsored plan, penalty-free; if you were at least 55 years old in the year you left your job. In between ages 55 and 59-1/2, therefore, you are better off keeping your money in a company plan, if you expect to take distributions.

Your life insurance should be considered, too. If your account in an employer-sponsored plan includes life insurance, you might want to keep your money in that plan in order to keep the policy in force. That is because you may find it costly to continue your life insurance after you leave the company plan. Especially if you are in poor health, you might not be able to buy needed coverage at a reasonable price.

In sum, you might decide against a rollover if (1) you live in a state with poor creditor protection for IRAs; (2) you need cash right away; (3) you do not want to manage your own retirement funds; (4) you intend to keep working after age 70-1/2; (5) you have taken or might take plan loans; (6) you are retiring between ages 55 and 59-1/2; or (7) you have vital life insurance inside your employer's plan. If none of those apply to you, an IRA rollover probably is the best choice.

Leading Roll

In some situations, IRAs are especially appealing. Suppose, for example, you are interested in a Roth IRA conversion. After five years and age 59-1/2, all withdrawals may be tax-free. Only traditional IRAs may be converted to a Roth IRA. Therefore, you must first rollover an employer's plan to an IRA, in order to subsequently convert to a Roth IRA. Keep in mind that Roth IRA conversions are permitted only if your income that year is not over $100,000. You will owe tax on all the deferred income when you convert an IRA to a Roth IRA.

In any case, always ask for a "trustee-to-trustee transfer" from your employer's plan to your IRA custodian. Keep your hands off the money being rolled over. If you handle the funds personally, you will face mandatory 20% withholding on the rollover.

Suppose you rollover a $500,000 account from your employer's plan and you take possession of the funds. Of your $500,000, $100,000 (20%) must be withheld. You will have to make up the difference with $100,000 from your own pocket to avoid owing income taxes and possibly a $10,000 (10%) penalty.

10% Solutions

As noted above, there are certain exceptions to the 10% penalty for IRA withdrawals before age 59-1/2. They include death (your beneficiary will not owe the penalty), disability, divorce, steep medical bills, higher education, and (for up to $10,000 worth of withdrawals) a first-time home purchase. In addition, the so-called "72(t)" rules provide a way to avoid a penalty. Under these rules, you can avoid a penalty if you take money from your IRA in "substantially equal periodic payments." These payments must go on for five years, or until age 59-1/2, whichever comes later. Once you get started with 72(t) withdrawals, if you do not keep them up until the five-year or age-59-1/2 mark, all of your cumulative withdrawals become subject to the 10% penalty, plus interest.

If you decide to take advantage of the 72(t) rules, you can choose among three methods:

Life expectancy (also known as the required minimum distribution) method. If your life expectancy is 35 years, for example, you would withdraw 1/35 of your IRA balance. The next year, you would withdraw 1/34 of the new balance. And so on. This method is chosen by people who want to minimize penalty-free withdrawals and leave as much as possible in the IRA.

Amortization and annuitization methods. These methods assume your IRA will grow at a certain rate. Therefore, the IRA is projected to become larger and you can take out greater amounts each year.

These two methods are used by people who want to maximize penalty-free withdrawals for living expenses. Generally, the amount you withdraw in Year One is the amount you will withdraw in each successive year.

Flex Plan

For some taxpayers, the IRS has approved a hybrid, "annual recalculation" method. That is, some IRA owners received permission to choose the amortization or the annuitization method, to get larger penalty-free distributions. Moreover, they can recalculate their distributions each year to rise or fall with their IRA balance.

In order to use such a hybrid method, here is what taxpayers were instructed:

1. Pick a method (typically, the amortization method), a valuation date, and a specific type of interest rate.

2. Re-set each variable (the IRA amount, life expectancy, and the interest rate) each year, on the same date.

3. Recalculate to determine the amount that can be distributed each year. This must be done every year, until five years or age 59-1/2, whichever comes later.

The hybrid method is appealing because you can take a relatively large amount from your IRA, penalty-free. If your IRA grows, so can your penalty-free distributions. However, if there is a stock market crash and your IRA shrinks, you can cut back and thus keep from stripping your IRA.

Required Reading

Another set of rules—and another penalty—affects *tardy withdrawals*. You must start to take distributions by April 1 of the year after you reach age 70-1/2. Very specific rules dictate how much you need to take out.

Once you reach that age, known as the required beginning date (RBD), there are minimum amounts you must withdraw each year and pay tax on. As long as you are alive and there is money left in your account, you will be required to continue to take these minimum distributions. You can take larger distributions from your retirement account, if you wish, but you must withdraw at least the minimum amounts each year. What is the penalty for not doing so? If you do not withdraw as much as you should, you face a 50% penalty!

Suppose you are 76 years old with $330,000 in your IRA. According to the IRS, you must withdraw at least 1/22 of your IRA this year, or $15,000. If you withdraw only $5,000, which would be a $10,000 shortfall; you would owe a $5,000 penalty—50% of the $10,000 shortfall.

For many people, that will not be a problem. In the example above, with a $330,000 IRA, 76-year-old Joe Madison needs to withdraw more than $15,000 per year for living expense, so he will not have to deal with any penalties.

Suppose, though, that 76-year-old Lisa Adams has the same $330,000 IRA but has other assets. She would prefer not to tap her IRA and pay the resulting income tax. How can Lisa withdraw as little as possible, to avoid a steep penalty, yet still maximize the tax deferral within her IRA?

Table Stakes

The IRS has made the calculation simpler by introducing a Uniform Distribution Table, which most people can use. However, if your beneficiary is a spouse who is more than ten years younger, you can use your actual joint life expectancies rather than the Uniform Distribution Table, which will be longer. Using a longer life expectancy means a smaller withdrawal and greater tax deferral.

Say you are 71 and your IRA beneficiary is your spouse, age 69. Under the table, the joint life expectancy would be 26.5 years. In this case, you could withdraw only 3.7736% (1/26.5) of the previous year-end IRA balance and still avoid a penalty. The same would be true if your spouse is 62, 66, 70, or older than you are.

However, if your spouse actually is 59 when you are 71, the joint life expectancy would really be 27.9 years, under the IRS tables. You could withdraw slightly less—3.5842%—from your plan with no penalty. (The tables can be found on Internet sites such as www.irahelp.com.)

Off To a Good Start

The above scenario illustrates the minimum required distribution (MRD) rules, which generally apply to IRAs and other tax-deferred accounts. Most people have to take a MRD after they reach age 70-1/2. Suppose, for example, you turn 70-1/2 in the first half of 2006. Later in 2006, you will reach your 71st birthday. Your first distribution must be taken by April 1 of the following year, 2007. Because you turned 71 in 2006, you would use the joint life expectancy for a 71-year-old. For your second required distribution, due by December 31, 2007, you would use the joint life expectancy for a 72-year-old. Each following year, you would have to take another distribution.

On the other hand, suppose you turn 70-1/2 in the second half of 2006, so you have your 70th birthday in 2006. You still have to take two distributions in 2007, by April 1 and December 31. Now, though, your required minimum distributions will use the life expectancies of a 70-year-old and a 71-year-old, respectively.

In both of these examples, you are taking two distributions in 2007. If you take two distributions the first year, the added income may push you into a higher tax bracket. Taking one distribution in 2006 and one in 2007 might result in a lower overall tax bill. In any case, the distribution you are required to take by December 31, 2007, would be based on a percentage of your IRA balance at year-end 2006 while your first distribution would be a percentage of your IRA balance at year-end 2005.

Going forward, the IRA distribution tables are based on the age you reach on your birthday during the calendar year. If you reach 75 in 2006, for example, that would be your age for calculating your required minimum withdrawal by December 31, 2006.

Under the Uniform Distribution Table, a 75-year-old with a beneficiary usually has a joint life expectancy of 22.9 years. In 2006, you would have to take out at least 4.3668% (1/22.9) of your IRA balance. That percentage would be applied to your year-end IRA balance, in 2005, and the resulting amount must be withdrawn by year-end 2006.

Heir Power

MRD rules also apply to inherited IRAs. Under the rules now in effect, the official "designated beneficiary" of an IRA will be determined on September 30 of the year following death. That is, if you inherit an IRA from someone who dies in 2006, the designated beneficiary of the IRA will not be determined until September 30, 2007. This does not mean, though, that a new beneficiary can be named after the IRA owner's death. What does it mean then? During this post-death period the designated beneficiary can be changed, but only to some other beneficiary or contingent beneficiary that was named by the IRA owner.

Suppose, for example, you are the primary beneficiary of an IRA. If you do not need the inheritance, you can disclaim in favor of your children, if they are the contingent beneficiaries. Disclaimers must be made in writing, within nine months of the IRA owner's death. Then your children could extend distributions over their longer life expectancy.

On the other hand, the final regulations explicitly state that an estate is not a designated beneficiary and thus is not eligible to stretch out distributions from an inherited IRA. This underscores the importance of naming a beneficiary and gives added significance to naming a contingent beneficiary.

What happens if you do not name an IRA beneficiary? Whoever inherits the account will have to withdraw more money, sooner, and pay more income tax. The same is true if you name your estate as the beneficiary. Thus, you should name one or more individuals as beneficiaries, on the form provided by the custodian or on a custom form you provide. If you have doubts about your beneficiary's ability to handle a large inheritance, you can name a trust as the beneficiary, then name your heirs as trust beneficiaries. If handled properly, setting up such a trust can permit your heirs to stretch out required withdrawals. You need to work with an experienced trust attorney, though.

Trickle-Down Triumph

With proper planning, ongoing tax deferral in the IRA you created can enrich your heirs. A poor plan, though, may rob your beneficiaries of a prime wealth building opportunity. In order to set the stage for maximum tax deferral after your death, a "cascading beneficiary" plan may be ideal. Keep in mind that your IRA will go to a designated beneficiary or beneficiaries at your death. No matter what you put in your will, it will not govern the disposition of your IRA. Therefore, it is vital that the proper paperwork is in place, outside of your will.

Chances are that you will set up your IRA with a bank, brokerage firm, mutual fund family, or insurance company that acts as the IRA custodian. This firm will have provided a beneficiary designation form when you opened the account; you probably had to work with a small card that left no room for special provisions.

Generally, these standard forms are designed for the convenience of the IRA custodian. At many firms, thousands of IRA beneficiary forms are handled by relatively unsophisticated personnel. Therefore, IRA custodians want to make things simple, for their own people. Such simplicity, though, may not serve the interests of your loved ones, after your death. To make the most of this extremely valuable asset, you must take an active role in selecting IRA beneficiaries.

A cascading beneficiary designation can give your survivors more flexibility as well as a chance to build extraordinary amounts of wealth. To get the desired result, you probably need to draw up your own beneficiary form, drafted by an attorney. On this form you can spell out your instructions, in some detail. Once it is complete, you can send in the customized form and ask for a receipt, acknowledging your instructions. Keep a copy of this paperwork with your will and let your IRA beneficiary know where it is located. If your IRA custodian refuses to accept your instructions, find a more cooperative custodian.

Go With the Flow

Here is how a cascading beneficiary plan might flow:

1. **Your spouse** probably will be the primary beneficiary of your IRA, if you are married. At your death, your spouse can claim the inherited IRA as his or her own and designate your children as the beneficiaries.

2. **Your children** can be named as secondary beneficiaries. This provides your surviving spouse with flexibility.

    Suppose, for example, your surviving spouse has sufficient wealth from other assets, aside from your IRA. Funds from your IRA will not be needed. In such a situation, if you have named your children as contingent beneficiaries, your spouse can disclaim. Then your children will inherit your IRA.

    An inherited IRA is subject to MRD rules, based on the life expectancy of the beneficiary. If your son inherits an IRA at age 47, the IRS gives him a 37-year life expectancy. Assuming he does not need more cash, he can take as little as 1/37 of the balance in Year One, leaving the other 36/37 to grow, tax-deferred. Each year, the percentage he is required to withdraw would increase slightly but 37 years of tax deferral can be extremely rewarding.

3. **Your grandchildren** can be tertiary beneficiaries, in case your children as well as your spouse disclaim. Their life expectations would be even longer, providing more tax deferral.

4. **Great-grandchildren**, if you have them, can be added to the list, in case your grandchildren disclaim.

Remember, the person who disclaims cannot direct the inheritance. He or she merely steps aside and the IRA will go to the next person in line, as specified on the beneficiary designation document.

Naming Names

The plan described above may have two advantages:

Income tax deferral. Your children and grandchildren will have longer life expectancies than your surviving spouse. If your spouse decides to disclaim, the younger heirs can stretch out minimum required withdrawals over a longer time period and get more benefit from the IRA's tax deferral.

Potential estate tax reduction. Disclaiming the IRA will keep that account from being in your surviving spouse's estate. If your survivor has ample assets, estate tax might be due at her death. Disclaiming the IRA will put the account into your taxable estate but the overall estate tax bill may be lower.

For this plan to work, you cannot designate "grandchildren" or "great-grand-children" as a class of beneficiaries. Each grandchild or great-grandchild must individually be named as a beneficiary. Ideally, you should revise your beneficiary form right after each birth, adding the newcomers by name.

The younger the beneficiaries, the greater the tax-deferred buildup. However, as long as some of the beneficiaries or contingent beneficiaries are minors, you should designate a trust as the IRA beneficiary and name the youngsters as beneficiaries of that trust.

Trust Tactics

If you are reluctant to name an individual as beneficiary of your IRA, you can name a trust as IRA beneficiary and also name the intended recipients as trust beneficiaries. Then the trustee can take money from the IRA and pass it through to the trust beneficiaries. In certain cases, such a plan makes sense. Rather than name a minor or an incompetent person or a spendthrift as IRA beneficiary, you would rather rely upon a responsible trustee.

Under IRS regulations, in order to achieve maximum tax deferral with a trust as IRA beneficiary, four elements must be in place:

1. The trust must be valid under state law.

2. The trust must be irrevocable. (You can use a revocable trust that becomes irrevocable after your death.)

3. The individual trust beneficiaries must be clearly identifiable.

4. Trust documents must be provided to the IRA custodian.

If all four conditions are met, the IRA may be distributed over the life expectancy of the trust beneficiary. Suppose, for example, Will Allen leaves his IRA to a trust and names his daughter Beth as trust beneficiary. After Will's death, Beth has a 21-year life expectancy so the IRA may be stretched out over 21 years, extending tax-deferred accumulation.

Contingency Plans

IRS regulations, however, may make it difficult to achieve such a desirable result with a trust as IRA beneficiary. In many cases, the IRS will insist that all but remote beneficiaries will be considered, for the purpose of determining a payout after your death. This may include some contingent or remainder beneficiaries.

Suppose Will not only named a trust as IRA beneficiary and his daughter as trust beneficiary. He also named his grandchildren as contingent trust beneficiaries while a charity was named to receive the remainder of what is in the trust, after the death of all these beneficiaries.

If the trust does not contain the right language, the IRA may have to be distributed over the shortest life expectancy among all the beneficiaries. In this example, that likely would be the charity, which has no life expectancy, so the IRA would fall under a five-year rule, requiring complete distribution within five years.

Fortunately, such results can be avoided with shrewd planning. You might structure a trust that you name as IRA beneficiary as a "conduit" trust. Such a trust might require that 100% of the IRA minimum distributions be immediately paid out to the trust beneficiaries.

That is, after your death minimum distributions must be made from an inherited IRA. If you leave a $1 million IRA and the first-year required distribution is 4%, then at least $40,000 must be withdrawn (and made subject to income tax) that year. If this $40,000 must immediately be paid out to the trust beneficiaries, the trust will be treated as a conduit and secondary beneficiaries will not be considered, for purposes of calculating life expectancy.

Going Separate Ways

An even better result might occur when multiple trust beneficiaries are named. Generally, distributions must be stretched over the age of the *oldest* beneficiary. Suppose Will Allen, in the above example, had named his daughter Carrie and his son Matt, along with Beth as trust beneficiaries. After his death Carrie—the oldest—has a 17-year life expectancy so the IRA must be paid out over 17 years.

In some circumstances, each of the children may be able to take distributions over his or her own life expectancy. The final regulations allow multiple IRA beneficiaries to extend tax deferral over their own life expectancies. If you name three children as IRA beneficiaries, each may be able to use his or her own life expectancy to withdraw the appropriate portion of the inherited IRA.

To achieve this result, separate shares must be created in the beneficiary designation form for the IRA. If so, by September 30th of the year following the year of the IRA owner's death, each beneficiary must establish a separate account and use his or her individual life expectancy for a withdrawal rate.

A similar result could occur in the above example, where Will Allen has named a trust as IRA beneficiary, with Carrie, Matt, and Beth as trust beneficiaries. Separate accounts must be established in the IRA owner's designated beneficiary form and the trust document.

Again, separate accounts should be established by September 30th of the year following the year of the IRA owner's death. This would allow the three trust beneficiaries to stretch out distributions over their own life expectancy, to the benefit of the younger beneficiaries.

Exclude Estates

Whether or not the above strategy is adopted, naming an estate as a trust beneficiary can be a huge mistake. Suppose that trust assets are to be payable to a beneficiary's estate if that beneficiary dies before reaching a certain age. Now the estate is among the beneficiaries and an estate, like a charity, has no life expectancy. In such a situation, if the IRA owner dies before the date he must begin to take minimum distributions, the IRA will have to be paid out within five years. If the owner dies after that date, distributions can be taken over his remaining life expectancy. In neither case can the distributions be stretched out over the beneficiary's life expectancy and there may be a substantial loss of tax-deferred growth. Therefore, you probably should avoid naming an estate as a backup beneficiary.

These pitfalls must be considered if you want to name a trust as IRA beneficiary. Chances are, if an IRA trust already is in your estate plan, it does not contain the language necessary for assuring a long stretch out. In that case, you might
want to change your IRA beneficiary designation, naming a newly-created trust
designed to comply with the new regulations. Work with a knowledgeable professional who has extensive experience in this intricate area of the tax law.

Maximize Minimums

Whether you name individual IRA beneficiaries or a trust, multi-generation IRA
planning may allow you to leave a large legacy. Assume, for example, that Chris
Jackson begins to take minimum required distribution with an IRA balance of $1
million, and that the IRA investments earn 10% per year.

Over the next 20 years, Chris and his wife Linda, who survives him, would
take out more than $2 million, taking minimum distributions under the current
IRS tables. Even after taking all those distributions, there would still be over $2
million in the IRA, which they can leave to their two children.

Say that one beneficiary is their son Kevin, who can take minimum distributions over his life expectancy. If he is 63 then, with a 20-year life expectancy, he
could take another $2 million from the inherited IRA.

In this example, suppose that the other beneficiary is their daughter Denise,
who decides to disclaim. Then Denise's share of the IRA will pass to her own
daughter Jan, who has been named a contingent beneficiary. Assuming that Jan is
28, with a 55-year life expectancy, she might withdraw more than $30 million
over the next half-century-plus, taking minimum distributions.

The net result? Thanks to extended tax deferral and compound earnings, a $1
million IRA may provide around $35 million to Chris, his spouse, and their
descendants.

It is true that an IRA might earn less than 10% per year, which is approxi-
mately the historic long-term return on U.S. equities, and also true that all withdrawals will be subject to income tax at ordinary rates. Even so, this type of tax
deferral plan can generate enormous wealth for your heirs.

Bridging the Generation Gap

You should realize that leaving an IRA to grandchildren, outright or in trust, may
trigger the generation-skipping transfer (GST) tax. If a grandparent-to-grand-
child IRA bequest is subject to estate tax and GST tax, most of the IRA's value

may be lost to the tax collectors if the IRA exceeds the GST exemption amount, which is $2 million in 2006.

However, even counting the effects of the GST tax, leaving your IRA to a grandchild still makes sense. That is especially true if the taxes can be paid from other sources, keeping the inherited IRA intact for tax-deferred future growth.

That is, your family might be better off paying the GST now, on a relatively small amount. If you try to avoid the GST tax by leaving the IRA to a child rather than a grandchild, more estate tax may be paid at the child's death, on a larger amount. For long-term wealth building, consider stretching IRA distributions as long as possible.

10

Protecting Disabled Dependents

✦

Special Concerns for Heirs with Special Needs

Some of your loved ones may have emotional or physical handicaps; in other cases, they may have succumbed to substance addiction. If these loved ones are younger than you are, and likely to survive you, providing for their ongoing care will be a prime concern. How can you protect those loved ones after you are no longer there for them? Yes, you might bequeath them adequate, even ample, resources. But if they are not capable of managing them and if they are vulnerable to predators, those assets may be dissipated, leaving your disabled survivors short of needed funds.

To avoid such a situation you must plan now, while you are able to do so. What should be in such a plan? To start, pay special attention to your life insurance needs. In case you should die prematurely, a disabled survivor may need extra amounts of financial support. However, buying adequate life insurance is just the first step. You also need to name a beneficiary to receive the proceeds. In some cases, the person with the disability will not be capable of handling such a large amount of money.

Time for a Trust

You might name your spouse as a beneficiary…but who will care for the disabled person after your spouse dies or becomes incapacitated? Often, the best way to provide for continuing care is to set up a trust. That is true whether or not the trust is funded with life insurance proceeds. A trust can remain in existence after your death. If a trust is created for the benefit of a disabled child, for example, money in that trust can be used to provide support far into the future. Extra planning may be needed if you are setting up a trust to help someone who is disabled. You will want to preserve the trust beneficiary's eligibility for government benefits, including:

Supplemental Security Income (SSI), administered by the Social Security Administration, which pays extra cash to the elderly and the disabled with limited assets and income.

Medicaid, a joint federal-state program that provides medical assistance to eligible parties, including low-income disabled individuals. Medicaid offers community medical services, home care services, and institutional care services.

Extra Helpful

SSI provides added benefits, in the form of a monthly cash stipend, for the aged (65 and older), the blind, and the disabled. To be eligible, someone must have few assets as well as scant income. In essence, an SSI recipient cannot hold more than $2,000 worth of savings accounts, checking accounts, stocks, bonds, real estate, jewelry, etc. (The limit is $3,000 for a couple.)

Some assets are not counted towards the $2,000 or $3,000 limits:

- A principal residence and the land it is on.

- A car with a retail value of $4,500 or less. However, more valuable cars may be excluded if they are (1) used for transportation to work or treatment of a medical problem or (2) modified for use by a handicapped person. In practice, many cars are excluded from the SSI limits.

- Burial funds up to $1,500 ($3,000 for a couple).

Just as having excess assets can disqualify a person from receiving SSI, income also can reduce or eliminate the SSI payment. The first $20 of monthly income will not affect SSI benefits; the same is true of the first $65 of earned monthly income ($85 if the person has no unearned income) and one-half of any additional earned income over that amount.

All-Encompassing Aid

Chapter 6 explained how Medicaid pays for many of the costs of long-term care. The same program provides far-reaching medical care to the needy. Again, Medicaid applicants have to observe certain rules on asset transfers; similar restrictions apply to SSI applicants. Once someone is accepted by Medicaid, he can see doctors, dentists, and therapists, with the program picking up the tab—everything from eyeglasses to prescription drugs will be covered. Medicaid will pay for health aides visiting at home and for hospital visits, too. In addition, some vital programs for the disabled are available only to people who are receiving SSI and Medicaid. However, people who have a certain amount of assets will not qualify for SSI and Medicaid and thus may be excluded from valuable benefits. If you give or bequeath assets directly to a loved one who is on SSI or Medicaid, he or she probably will be taken off public assistance until that wealth is all spent. Then the process of re-qualifying for benefits has to begin anew.

Something Special

How can you provide for a loved one without jeopardizing their public assistance? If you have a relatively small estate, the most practical strategy is to cut the disabled child out of your will. Leave his share to one or more of your other children, the ones you think most likely to care for their disabled brother.

For sizable estates, the best solution may be to put money in trust for disabled dependents but to do so in a manner that will not impair their eligibility for public assistance. That is, you might create a "special needs" trust, sometimes called a "supplemental needs" trust. Properly drafted, a special needs trust can enhance the beneficiary's lifestyle by providing certain items, from eyeglasses to vacations, while retaining his eligibility for public assistance benefits.

What else might a special needs trust provide to a disabled beneficiary? Educational programs, entertainment, companions, aides, home improvements, transportation, medical care not covered by Medicaid. The list can go on, as long as the trustee is determined to act in the beneficiary's best interests.

Distributions from the trust for such purposes may result in taxable income to the beneficiary. However, it may be the case that the beneficiary will have little other income, especially if he or she is eligible for SSI benefits; if so, distributions from the trust effectively will be tax-free. A special needs trust provides an added benefit because trust funds generally cannot be seized by a creditor or a spouse in a divorce action.

In order to meet its objectives, this type of trust must be carefully worded so that it will not pay for basic needs (food and shelter), which will remain the responsibility of government agencies. After the basics have been provided, the trustee can use the money in the trust to provide "extras" not covered by SSI or Medicaid. To maximize the advantage of a special needs trust, cash distributions to the beneficiary should be discouraged if not prohibited. Such distributions will reduce benefits, under the formula described above. In addition, a "spendthrift" clause can prevent the trust beneficiary from assigning or pledging trust assets.

Word Perfect

In order to keep public agencies from denying benefits to your disabled dependent, the language of the trust should specifically state that the trustee has the right to distribute trust assets in such a way that they will supplement but not supplant government benefits. You also may want to name other trusts beneficiaries and give the trustee the right, but not the obligation, to distribute trust funds among them. This may prevent SSI from claiming the trust assets really belong to the disabled individual.

If you are setting up a trust for a loved one, it is vital that you pick the right trustee. You need someone who will be sympathetic to the beneficiary's situation, yet also prudent about handling the trust funds. When you create a trust, you set the ground rules for the trustee. Generally, you will want the trustee to have a great deal of discretion on distributing trust income and principal in order to meet the beneficiary's needs. Often, it is better not to name just one trustee. You should name one or two successor or replacement trustees in case your first choice is unwilling or unable to serve. In addition, there should be some procedure for selecting future trustees. You might say, for example, that the trust department of a local bank will take over after the trust has gone through all the individual trustees that you have named.

If you decide to create a special needs trust, it can go into effect at your death. Alternatively, creating such a trust while you are alive can let you see how it is working. Moreover, gifts to fund the trust can remove assets from your taxable estate.

According to Plan

What if you have accumulated most of your net worth in your retirement plan? You can name a trust as the beneficiary of the retirement plan account. Thus, if you have created a trust for the benefit of a disabled dependent (and perhaps for other beneficiaries as well), that trust also can serve as the beneficiary of your IRA. After your death, the trustee can stretch withdrawals over the life expectancy of the oldest trust beneficiary, prolonging the tax deferral and providing more wealth for a loved one who may truly need it.

11

Retirement Housing

♦

Trading Places

For some seniors, retirement means more than a change in lifestyle: it also means a change of address. You might want to move to a different home, or even to a different state. Relocating in retirement may be attractive, for any of several reasons. You might want to be near loved ones, for example, or you may choose a warm-weather site where you won't have to worry about shoveling snow any more. Some areas of the country may have more affordable real estate and a lower cost of living than the state you currently call home.

Tax reduction is another major concern for retirees who are ready to relocate. If you are on a fixed income, you might choose a state without an income tax over a high-tax state. Before you make a move, though, check into the total picture. Some "high-tax" states have breaks for seniors, such as tax exemptions for pensions and Social Security benefits. "Low-tax" states may have hefty property taxes or other levies such as an intangibles tax. Therefore, you should investigate the entire tax picture before making a move.

This evaluation also should include estate tax. As mentioned in Chapter 4, some states are increasing taxes on estates or on heirs, as an offset to reduced revenue from federal estate tax. If you expect to leave a large estate, relocating can save substantial amounts for your family. According to one estimate, an Illinois resident dying with a $20 million estate in 2005 could have saved $1.2 million if the decedent had moved to a state such as Florida, where estate taxes do not have the same bite. Thus, changing "domicile" can pay off, in lower estate tax as well as income tax. However, your old state may still come after you for tax, while you are alive, and then pursue your estate after your death.

How can you show that you have really moved to a low-tax state? There is no magic formula but following these steps will strengthen your case:

- Spend more than half the year in your new state.

- In your old state, move to a house or apartment that is smaller than the one in your new state. Even better, relinquish any residence in your old state.

- Avoid part-time or free-lance work that will result in payments from companies based in your old state.

- File a final income tax return for your old state.

- Going forward, file income tax returns for your new state (if it has an income tax). File only non-resident returns with your old state, if they are required.

- Put your new state's address on all tax returns.

- File your federal income tax returns with the IRS Service Center for your new state.

- Register to vote in your new state and vote regularly in that state.

- Apply for a driver's license in your new state.

- Register your vehicles in your new state.

- Whenever you apply for or renew a federal document, such as a passport, put down your new state as your residence.

- Execute a new will (and a revocable trust, if that is part of your estate plan), declaring yourself a resident of your new state.

Relative Strength

Although taxes certainly will be a factor, other issues may determine whether relocation really is a practical choice. Although there are exceptions, some people will not move just to save taxes. There is often another reason to be in the new state—many people who relocate have children or a second home in the other state.

Sometimes, though, the choice is between children in the old state and a second home in the new state. Take the example of Louis A., a widower in his 80s. He is physically able to take care of himself. His children are in New York, where Louis now lives, but they do not mind the thought of going to Florida occasionally, in the winter, to see how he is doing.

Louis already has a condo in Florida as well as a house in New York. He has been spending four to five months each year in Florida but now he expects to spend more than six months there. In addition, Louis has relocated his brokerage account and his bank accounts to Florida. He is doing what he can so that the focal point of his life is Florida, not New York.

Conversely, family concerns may tilt the scales against relocating. Michael B., for example, has an extremely large estate but no plans to move to an estate tax haven. Michael is a widower, too, but he is more incapacitated. His children are concerned that they will have to fly down to Florida from the Northeast all the time, if he is ill. Thus, this family is willing to pay the extra estate tax in order to keep their father within easy reach, for most of the year.

Seeking the Simpler Life

Whether you move to a new state or stay close to home, by the time you retire you may have reached the point where you prefer to have fewer responsibilities. If so, you may be interested in moving to a retirement community that takes over some of the chores. Generally, there are three main issues you need to consider if you are in the market for a retirement community.

First, there is the geographical issue. Some retirees relocate to live in a community, only to come back in a year or two. Why do retirees return to the old neighborhood? Mainly because of family reasons—some people do not realize how much they will miss being close to their relatives. Frequently, retirees who relocate think that children or grandchildren will come down on a regular basis just to use the pool in the new community. That is seldom the case, though. Relatives may not be willing to visit unless the retirees provide the airplane tickets.

There may be other drawbacks to relocation. For example, Northerners may not realize how long the summer can be in the South or Southwest, and how hot it is. Medical care becomes a vital concern, too. People must find new doctors when they relocate, so they have to make adjustments, yet at this time of their lives they may have an increasing need for health care.

Second, you have to choose among the different varieties of retirement communities that are available. There are some that appeal mainly to younger retirees: those in their 60s. These communities tend to feature golf courses, other recreational facilities, and social activities. Such communities may be especially appealing to healthy retirees who want to do a good bit of traveling. You can just pick up and go whenever you want, without worrying about the upkeep on your home. The community is responsible for the maintenance of the grounds and common areas—all you have to do is pay a maintenance charge. Even in such communities, where healthy retirees live independently, some medical care may be available. There might be a doctor or nurse on call 24 hours a day. That type of service may be very comforting because you will have access to skilled care in case of an emergency.

Other types of communities may be called multistage or continuing care communities. Some residents are in good health, living independently, as described above. The same community, though, will have assisted living facilities for those who need a modest amount of help (see below). Residents at this level might need someone to help them bathe, dress, or keep the house clean. They might be entitled to one or two meals a day in a common dining area.

Finally, such communities will have true nursing home facilities, for people who need custodial care on a full-time basis. In theory, once you enter this type of facility you can stay there for the rest of your life, as you become less able to care for yourself. You should be aware, though, that the environment is much different in a community offering a substantial amount of health care than it is in a community where most people are active. There will be more health care workers and infirm residents; make sure you are aware of this environment before moving in.

Third, the financial arrangements retirees must make in order to move into a community are vital. In some cases residents make a straightforward real estate decision: they buy a house or a condo and plan to sell it later, or have their heirs sell it. Other retirement communities are pure rentals: residents pay so much per month for the right to live there. The greater the level of service desired, the higher the monthly charge.

Other types of communities offer a hybrid approach. Residents pay an upfront fee that is not exactly a home purchase. In addition, they still pay a hefty monthly fee, but one that is purportedly lower than it would have been for a comparable level of service, without the initial charge. In such communities, there is usually some provision for a refund or partial refund of the initial fee when the resident dies or moves out. A few communities still refuse to pay any refunds and those communities probably should be avoided.

Naturally, it is important to read any contract carefully before signing, to see exactly what you will be paying and what you will be getting. Multistage communities, though, may require even greater scrutiny than a straight real estate purchase or rental. Married couples especially will want to know what happens if one spouse has to move into a long-term care facility. Can the other spouse stay in their home? Will a move to a smaller, less expensive living unit be permitted, or even required?

Similarly, single residents should ask what will happen if they need assisted living or nursing home care. In some cases, the move is irreversible—the resident will not be allowed back in the old home and a new resident will move in. There may be some rationale to such a rule but you should know about it in advance.

Wait Control

Considering that you may be choosing a home for the rest of your life, you should look into such details carefully before making any decisions. One good sign is the presence of a long waiting list for a community. Not only does this mean that a community is popular with residents, it also indicates that there is a resale market for properties there, if you buy a home.

One viable strategy: do your homework in advance. If you find a community with a two-year waiting list, for example, sign up when you are two years from your desired move-in date. Typically, there are little or no costs involved in getting on a waiting list. If your turn comes up and you are not ready to move in, you can remove yourself from the list or ask to go back to the end of the line.

What other strategies can help you obtain a spot in a prized retirement community?

Start early. Do your investigation when you are healthy and energetic.

Work your network. Ask friends, relatives, and local senior citizen's groups for leads to communities with good reputations and for warnings about trouble spots.

Be realistic about money. Compare the costs you will incur at a retirement community with your current living expenses.

Kick the tires. Visit a community before moving in. Find out if the community is accessible to local stores, entertainment centers, and houses of worship. Economical van or bus service will be a huge plus if you stay in a community beyond the age when you can drive your own car.

Finally, ask for a community's most recent financial statements (audited by an independent professional) and have them evaluated by your own advisor. Even the most attractive community will not look as good if it goes bankrupt just when you are in need of extensive care.

Medical Matters

Beyond basic money matters, you should look into the details of promised health care, which is included in the package at many continuing care communities. Some communities may have a registered nurse on-premises 24 hours a day, every day. In other communities, the nurse's hours may be limited to 9-5 on weekdays. Find out what nursing services are available and, if there are gaps, what fallbacks the community provides.

Similarly, you should find out if a community has arrangements with a nearby hospital or clinic for medical situations that require a physician rather than a registered nurse. An affiliation with a renowned medical center may be extremely reassuring.

Of course, one of the main reasons for paying a sizable upfront fee for admission to a continuing care community is to gain access to nursing home care. If you eventually need custodial care, the community's nursing facilities will be available. In some communities, residents are required to buy long-term care insurance to help cover the costs.

Nevertheless, all long-term care is not equal so you should inspect those facilities carefully. Are there enough nursing beds to serve all those who need care? What happens if there is a shortage? If a married couple lives in a community, what extra costs will be involved if one spouse needs nursing care while the other remains in their former residence?

Get answers to these questions before you pay any entrance fees. A community's nursing facilities should include a separate wing for patients with Alzheimer's or other forms of dementia. Such people need specialized care; they may disrupt other patients if they all live together.

While you certainly should look at a community's long-term care facilities, you should not dwell on them. If you approach a place with the idea that this is "the end of the line," you will not be very eager to move in. On the other hand, if you focus on the activities and the amenities, you will be more receptive towards the idea of living in such a community. In truth, such communities may be ideal for seniors, thanks to all the companionship they can provide. Widespread camaraderie may be the best medicine for preventing a disabling illness and an ensuing long nursing home stay.

Not all retirement communities offer the same activities. Before you move in, check to see if your favorite pursuits—tennis, fishing, crafts, bridge—will be available. If you love to dance, go to a dance and see what it is like.

You also should inquire about transportation because many retirees reach a point where they no longer can drive a car. Many communities offer bus or van service to movie theaters, shopping centers, medical offices, and so on.

No matter how much research you do, there is no guarantee of happiness at any given retirement community. You should know in advance how much of your deposit you will forfeit by moving out. Today, many retirement communities offer 90-day trial periods, during which you can get your full deposit back if you are not satisfied.

You also should not have to worry about being dispossessed if you live until 120 and your money runs out. Ask whether a retirement community has a "benevolent fund" to take care of residents who have become destitute. A retirement community may well be the last place you will ever live. Spend the time and effort to increase the chances your retirement will always be truly comfortable.

Help Wanted

The idea of living in a retirement community with a pool, spa, exercise facilities, etc., may seem inviting. However, as you grow older, living independently might no longer be possible. Having someone come in to help probably will be the first choice, but that is not always practical. If home care is not a reasonable option, assisted living may turn out to be less expensive and more appealing than moving into a nursing home.

The term assisted living refers to a level of aid provided to those who need some help with day-to-day living but who do not need full-time nursing care. In effect, assisted living comes between one's own home and a nursing home.

Virtually any type of real estate may be an assisted living facility (ALF). You can find assisted living in apartment buildings, large or small, or converted single-family homes. So what do ALFs have in common? They provide special services not found in regular rental units, such as:

- Meals served in a common dining area

- Housekeeping

- Transportation to stores, medical appointments

- Assistance with laundry, bathing, dressing, etc.

- Medication management

- Social and recreational activities

While it is true that assisted living facilities may run the gamut, in terms of the residents' health and the services they can expect, the most common arrangement might be a single-room apartment with no stove or hot plate. The goal is to keep fire out of the apartments.

Such arrangements are deemed necessary for the safety of the residents, who are generally females, over 80, living close to a son or a daughter. Their physical well-being has declined and they need more help than their children can provide. In addition, they enjoy the added sociability. In fact, the main benefits of assisted living may well be socialization and help to make sure residents take needed medicine.

Cheaper, Not Cheap

Assisted living is not inexpensive but it is generally less costly than the full-time care provided in a nursing home. As mentioned in Chapter 6, the average cost of a nursing home in the U.S. is around $180 per day, more than $5,000 per month. In some areas, costs run into six figures per year.

For ALFs, the average cost is much lower, around $2,800 per month. It is true that assisted living costs may be greater than the average, depending on the services you choose, but ALF residents generally pay less than they would in a nursing home.

On the other hand, most assisted living costs are paid privately, rather than covered by public funds. You usually cannot rely on Medicaid, which pays nursing home costs for impoverished residents. Moreover, the amount you will be paying when you first enter an ALF is likely to climb over the years, perhaps by a great deal.

Therefore, if you are considering an ALF you should look at price increases over the past three to five years to get some idea of how future costs may rise. Also, if the facility is affiliated with a church or charity, which often is the case, you should find out if ongoing contributions will be expected and, if so, how much.

Although assisted living can be expensive, you will also enjoy some cost savings by moving from a house to an ALF. Once you move to an ALF, you will not pay property tax any longer. You will not have the other expenses of maintaining a house, such as hiring someone to shovel snow or rake leaves. Such savings, along with having the use of the proceeds from selling your house, may offset the costs of assisted living.

House Hunting

Because ALF residents usually are responsible for paying their own way, rather than relying upon public assistance, it is vital to shop carefully among the various alternatives before making any commitments. There is a great deal of diversity among ALFs. Some ALFs are low-budget properties while others are luxurious; many fall in-between. There are ALFs with special wings for dementia patients, designed to provide more safety.

Increasingly, some ALFs are positioning themselves to serve special markets. They may have kosher kitchens; they might be largely occupied by a particular ethnic group; some are near college campuses in order to attract alumni.

When you look for an ALF where you will feel comfortable, you also should investigate the payment plans. There are three common rate structures. Some facilities charge a flat rate each month. Others have three tiers, with tiers two and three more expensive than tier one, along with more services. Still others charge a base rate and add on fees if more services are required. Recently, the flat-fee approach has been losing ground to the other models.

Pick Of the Pack

Besides cost, other factors should be considered when choosing an ALF. You may want to be close to friends and family, for example. In addition, the helpfulness of the facility's employees is likely to be a crucial concern. Similarly, it will be vital to get along with your would-be neighbors.

The children of assisted living residents may prefer a facility close to where they live or work. Caregivers often receive calls from residents, with urgent requests to come and help. Being nearby can make a huge difference.

Therefore, you should investigate an ALF you are considering before making any commitments. Visit at different times and different days of the week to see whether you have found a place where you will enjoy living.

All in the Family

What if the ALF you have picked is more expensive than you had hoped to pay, if you choose the services you would like? Many assisted living residents get some financing from other family members. Indeed, some financial institutions offer loan programs in which several children can personally guarantee a loan to help pay for a parent's assisted living.

Tax breaks also can help to make ALFs more affordable. Assisted living outlays may be deductible medical expenses. Although there are no specific IRS or court rulings on assisted living, there are many rulings supporting deductions where the primary purpose of the expense is to get care. In assisted living, that is the norm.

If a middle-aged son or daughter provides the funds for a parent's assisted living, those outlays might be deductible medical expenses. In some cases, a dependency deduction can be claimed.

Insurance Insights

As explained in Chapter 6, many people buy long-term care (LTC) insurance to help offset future costs of nursing home or at-home care. If you are in the market for LTC insurance, make sure any policy you buy also will cover assisted living. LTC policies generally pay for care, not for living expenses, so a policy that covers assisted living may pay part of the monthly bill.

However, many residents in ALFs, especially those with minor cognitive problems, may not be sufficiently incapacitated to trigger benefits under most LTC insurance policies. Often, seniors and their children will make the decision to move to assisted living, thinking that their LTC care insurance will pay for the care, only to find out their claim is denied. If you have LTC coverage, make sure that you have the ability to pay the costs out-of-pocket, not only during the elimination period but during any claims denial and appeal process.

In some cases, LTC insurance will not pay at all, in an ALF setting. Thus, you should review any LTC policy you already own, especially home-health-care-only policies, nursing-home-only policies, or any policy issued before 1997. If assisted living coverage is not included, ask the insurer if that coverage can be added and, if so, at what cost.

Whether or not you have insurance coverage, you may not stay in an ALF indefinitely. On average, people stay less than two years before they need to move on to a nursing home for even more care. Nevertheless, the longer you can get by with just an assist, rather than full-time supervision, the more enjoyable your home life may be.

12

Charitable Thoughts

◆

Charity Begins at Home

Many seniors who have accumulated assets during their lives want to "give something back," as the saying goes. If you have ample funds for yourself and your spouse as well as a sufficient inheritance to pass on to other loved ones, you may be interested in making a substantial donation to a favorite charity, school, or not-for-profit organization.

The tax laws offer significant benefits for charitable contributions so you can do well while doing good. If you itemize deductions on Schedule A of your federal tax return, you can deduct charitable donations. There are some restrictions, though. Gifts that you make to public charities (that is, not to private foundations) cannot exceed 50% of your adjusted gross income (AGI). Moreover, donations of appreciated property (see below) cannot exceed 30% of your AGI for gifts to public charities. Suppose you expect your AGI this year to be $100,000. You can deduct charitable donations of up to $30,000 worth of appreciated property. If you donate the maximum $30,000 worth of appreciated property to charity, you also can donate up to $20,000 in cash and get a full first-year write-off. That would put you at $50,000 worth of charitable contributions, or 50% of your AGI. Any charitable donations you cannot deduct this year can be carried forward for up to five years. Each year, the same percentage-of-AGI limits apply.

Charitable deductions are permitted under the alternative minimum tax (AMT) rules. However, high-bracket taxpayers making large charitable contributions may reduce their regular income tax by so much that the AMT will come into play. Thus, you should meet periodically with your tax advisor to see how much you can effectively donate to charity each year.

Better Than Cash

If those are the ground rules, what are the fine points? Perhaps most important, you should look over your portfolio before you start writing checks.

Say you want to make $30,000 worth of charitable contributions this year and your tax advisor tells you that amount will be fully deductible. You can simply write $30,000 worth of checks to your favorite charities. However, you will probably be better off donating appreciated securities instead of cash. You can get a deduction for the full value of appreciated assets, as long as they have been held more than one year before the donation. The true benefit: your unpaid capital gain tax obligation disappears.

Suppose you hold stock you bought many years ago for $10,000, now trading at $30,000. Thus, you have a $20,000 unrealized gain. At a 15% federal tax rate on long-term gains, you would owe $3,000 in tax if you sold all the shares. Therefore, this holding is really worth only $27,000 to you, after-tax. By donating the shares, you can get a $30,000 deduction by giving away assets that really are worth only $27,000 to you. Yet the charity can sell the shares and retain all $30,000, because charities generally avoid income tax.

Easy Does It

In order to donate appreciated stocks, mutual fund shares, or other securities, here is all you have to do:

1. Call the charity and get its brokerage account number.

2. Call your own broker or your mutual fund company and explain what you want to do, providing the charity's account number.

3. Follow up by fax or phone to confirm the transaction.

Be sure not to donate securities held in an IRA, SEP, or other tax-deferred retirement plan. Under current tax law, the value of the shares donated to charity will be considered taxable income to you, at ordinary income rates. Instead, donate appreciated securities held in a taxable account, which will not trigger any income tax.

Another foolish step is donating securities selling at a loss. You should sell those securities instead, to take a tax loss, and donate the cash to charity.

More, Not Merrier

The above procedure for donating appreciated securities probably will work fine if you are making one $30,000 donation, or a few large donations. However, if you intend to make, donations of $3,000 each to 10 different charities, the paperwork involved can be daunting. For multiple donations of this nature, you might prefer to use a donor-advised fund (DAF). Many local community foundations sponsor DAFs. Or, you can invest through major financial firms such as Fidelity, Vanguard, and Schwab. When you use a DAF, you can make one substantial upfront contribution (cash, securities, or other assets). At that time, you can deduct this contribution as a donation to a public charity. Subsequently, at your own pace you can specify "grants" from the DAF to various charities. Thus, you can deduct now and deal with simpler paperwork later.

Suppose, for example, you donate $30,000 worth of appreciated stock to your local community foundation's DAF in 2006. The DAF is treated as a charity so it can sell the shares without owing any tax. You will have the full $30,000 in your account. Assuming that you comply with the AGI limits, you can take a $30,000 deduction for 2006. Going forward, you might notify the fund in January 2007 that you would like to donate $3,000 to your alma mater and $3,000 to a disabled veterans' group. Grants will be made to the specified recipients in your name so you will get the appropriate recognition.

Other grants can be made in the future, perhaps years from now. You can add to the account, if you would like. In the meantime, funds that are yet to be donated will be invested; investment earnings will be untaxed and can add to the amount available for future contributions. What's more, contributing to a donor-advised fund may be particularly effective if you have unusually large taxable income this year. You can get an upfront write-off to offset the extra income while you can fulfill your charitable commitments over a period of years. Some donor-advised funds impose a management fee for assets yet to be given to charity. Before donating, make sure the advantages you will enjoy justify the fees you will pay.

Putting On the Brakes

Besides cash and securities, other items may be donated to generate tax deductions. Clothing, collectibles, even life insurance policies that you no longer need may help a favored cause while trimming your tax bill. However, you should be cautious about donating autos to charity. The IRS has announced it will look hard at the values claimed for such donations. Again, you are probably better off selling the car and giving cash to charity.

For small gifts of goods, you can assign your own valuations without having to show receipts. Larger gifts require a paper trail, though:

- For a contribution of $250 or more, you must get a written receipt of your donation from the charity.

- For a donation of more than $500 worth of goods, you must include Form 8283 with your tax return, providing details about your gift.

- If you claim a deduction of more than $5,000 for any one item, you must have a qualified appraiser provide a valuation that you attach to Form 8283.

If you are donating art or other collectibles, you will need a record showing that the items are being used for the charity's primary purpose, to get a full deduction. For example, donating a painting that a university uses in art appreciation courses will provide a deduction for the painting's full value. That might not be the case, though, if the university just auctions off your painting as a fundraiser.

Give And Take

Some types of charitable contributions can provide more than good feelings and tax deductions: they offer cash flow, too. With a charitable gift annuity (CGA), for example, you can:

- Receive an immediate income tax deduction;

- Lock in guaranteed lifetime income for yourself and perhaps your spouse;

- Remove assets from your taxable estate with no gift tax consequences; and

- Enjoy the satisfaction of making a charitable contribution as well as the recognition that comes with it.

As the name suggests, with a CGA you make a gift to a charity or nonprofit organization. In turn, the recipient promises a stream of cash flow. The payments may continue over your lifetime, no matter how long you live, or the cash may keep flowing while either you or your spouse is alive. (Someone besides you or your spouse can be named as an annuitant or co-annuitant but gift tax liability may be incurred if payments are going to your son or your niece.)

Payments are fixed. Many charities use a table supplied by the American Council on Gift Annuities (ACGA) to set rates. The older you are when you enter into the contract, the higher your fixed payment will be. For example, if your nearest birthday is 65, when you agree to a CGA, you might receive 6%: $6,000 per year on a $100,000 CGA. If you wait until age 80, when your life expectancy is shorter, you might receive $8,000 per year on a $100,000 CGA.

Annuities covering two lives will pay less. A 65-year-old donor with a 60-year-old spouse, for example, might receive only 5.5% per year while a couple aged 75 and 80 might receive 6.6%. The rates you would get on a CGA are lower than the rates you would receive from a purely commercial annuity from an insurance company. While you give up some income with a CGA, you will support a favored cause and enjoy tax benefits. Even so, CGA rates are probably higher than the dividends or interest you would receive from a portfolio of stocks or bonds so this type of contract may appeal to retirees living on a fixed income. In essence, CGAs provide a means to tap principal as well as investment income.

Sweet Charity

With any form of annuity you acquire, the money received will be partially a tax-free return of principal and partially ordinary income. That is the case with a CGA. If the donation is made with appreciated assets held for more than one year, some of the income will be favorably taxed as a long-term capital gain.

With a CGA, you will get an immediate charitable deduction, too. When you enter into the agreement, the present value of the annuity is computed, based on interest rate tables provided by the IRS. This value is subtracted from the fair market value of the property donated and the difference may be taken as an immediate income tax deduction.

If you donate appreciated assets held more than a year, the current value will be included in this calculation, increasing your upfront deduction. Depending on current interest rates, donors in their 60s and 70s might qualify for upfront deductions of 35%-45%, on a single-life CGA.

With a $100,000 CGA, that would be a charitable deduction between $35,000 and $45,000. (These numbers are approximate and will change as interest rates fluctuate.) Older donors will get a higher write-off; the deduction will be lower if the CGA covers two lives.

Flex Plans

Some of the benefits offered by CGAs also can be provided by charitable remainder trusts (CRTs). After creating a CRT and transferring assets into the trust, you can specify a stream of payments to a beneficiary or beneficiaries you name. For example, you can name yourself and your spouse as the individual beneficiaries. The trust can be instructed to make payments as long as either is alive. When the individual beneficiaries no longer are receiving cash flow, the assets left in the trust (the "remainder") go to a charity or charities you have named. Again, you will get an immediate tax deduction. Under the tax code, you must structure the arrangement so that the present value of the future charitable gift is at least 10% of the amount transferred. With a $200,000 transfer, your charitable gift (and the resulting deduction) must be at least $20,000.

With a CRT, you have considerable flexibility as to the payment stream you can get. Possibilities include:

Annuity Trust. Here, you will get fixed payments. Each year, you must receive at least 5% of the amount you originally contributed. With a $200,000 transfer to the CRT, your fixed payment must be at least $10,000 a year.

Unitrust: Here, you get a fixed percentage of trust assets, determined each year. Again, that percentage must be at least 5% of trust assets. With a unitrust, payouts can grow or decrease if the trust assets earn more or less than the unitrust percentage.

Deferred CRT: If you do not need current income a NIMCRUT (net income with makeup charitable remainder unitrust) might be used. A NIMCRUT can be designed to pay out little now but more later, perhaps after you no longer have earned income.

For all types of CRTs, the IRS has indicated it does not like annual payouts to be extremely high, such as 50%. As a practical matter, the 10% rule mentioned above puts a cap on the payment you can specify. Often, though, if you wish to receive ample cash flow, an 8% or 9% payout will work.

Annuity or Trust?

Thus, both a CGA and CRT can give you an upfront deduction and lifelong income as well as enabling you to benefit a favorite charity. How do they compare?

Benefits of charitable gift annuities: A CGA generally is simpler and less expensive to create and maintain than a CRT. Many nonprofit institutions will make annuity arrangements for contributors. Also, the annuity payments are the legal liability of the charity issuing the contract, which is not the case with a CRT. Thus, future payments are secure if they are the responsibility of a financially-solid organization.

Another approach, offered by some charities, is a "pooled income fund." Here, donors contribute cash or securities to a fund, in exchange for lifelong payments. Again, there is a partial upfront deduction.

Compared with CGAs, pooled income funds offer variable rather than fixed returns, and the payout might be lower. Minimum contributions to a pooled fund might be as low as $10,000, so these vehicles can be suitable for relatively small donations.

Benefits of charitable remainder trusts: Although CRTs are more expensive than CGAs, they leave more control in the hands of you, the donor. For example, you can change the charitable beneficiary. There is more flexibility with a CRT, too. You can design a CRT so that payments will increase over time, if investment performance is sound, while CGA payments remain fixed.

Moreover, not all charitable organizations have CGA or pooled income programs so a CRT may be the only viable way to get an upfront deduction and ongoing cash flow while making a donation to the charity of your choice. If a CGA is available, though, it may be the best choice if you are concerned with cost saving, simplicity, and secure cash flow.

Putting Charity Last

As mentioned above, making charitable contributions of securities held in an IRA is not a good strategy because the value of the shares donated to charity will be considered taxable income to you. Similarly, if you donate cash from your IRA, the donation will be treated as a taxable withdrawal from your IRA.

If you have charitable intentions in your estate planning, though, you should shift into reverse. Make bequests from your IRA or another tax-deferred retirement account. With such a strategy, the deferred income tax can be avoided. In addition, you may be able to pass on appreciated assets to other heirs who will inherit with a tax-saving basis step-up.

Suppose, for example, Richard Adams has a total estate of $3 million. Half of that is in an IRA and the other half is in highly-appreciated securities and real estate. Richard wants to leave $1.5 million to his children and $1.5 million to various charities.

If the appreciated assets are left to charity while the IRA goes to the children, no federal estate tax will be due, under current law, assuming Richard dies before 2011. With this plan, though, the children eventually will have to pay income tax on the IRA money as it comes out. At a 35% rate, the federal income tax bill could be over $500,000.

A better approach would be to leave the IRA to charity and the appreciated assets to the children. Again, there will be no estate tax but the children will inherit the appreciated assets with a step-up in basis, under current law. If the children decide to sell those assets, they will not owe any capital gains tax on all the appreciation during Richard's lifetime. Thus, the latter approach passes on the estate completely tax-free, saving hundreds of thousands of dollars in taxes.

Alternate Endings

If you decide to follow this path, there are four methods you can use to make charitable bequests from your retirement plan:

- Leave your IRA directly to charity.

- Leave your IRA to your spouse, who will leave it to charity at his or her death.

- Leave your IRA to a trust for your spouse, with the trust principal ultimately going to charity.

- Leave your IRA to a CRT, naming the charity as the recipient of the remainder interest.

Generally, leaving your money directly to charity is most suitable if you are not married or if the bequest is relatively small in relation to your entire estate. In other situations, your spouse may not want to give up the IRA to charity. As for the other methods, if you are confident that your spouse always will be able to handle the IRA wisely, and make the appropriate charitable bequest, the IRA simply can be left to your spouse. In many situations, though, you will be better off using a trust, which can provide control and protection.

The tax code permits you to create a trust where the surviving spouse gets all the income while the first spouse to die gets to name the ultimate beneficiary, which can be a charity. No federal estate tax will be due at the first death. In case of need, the trustee can distribute more funds to the surviving spouse. At the survivor's death, whatever remains in the IRA goes to the charity you have named, tax-free.

Alternatively, if you want to limit the survivor's income, in order to provide more to charity, a CRT may be appropriate. With a CRT, your surviving spouse's income will be a fixed amount or a fixed percentage of CRT assets.

If you want to name children or grandchildren to also receive income from the trust, a CRT would be more suitable. In this scenario, though, a present value will be placed on the projected future income to younger generations and that amount may be subject to estate tax. A CRT also may result in speedier distributions from an inherited IRA so some tax deferral may be lost.

Happy Endings

Financial survival can be a formidable task for seniors. The task can be made easier with knowledge, such as the information provided above. Perhaps most important, successful senior planning should really be a family effort, with all parties sharing in the responsibilities.

In affluence or in need, the entire planning process will be more viable if there is communication between the generations. When they first retire, seniors should inform their children about their finances. As part of this communications effort, tell your heirs exactly what you have in mind for your future, should the time come when you are unable to speak for yourself. The more communication there is between children and parents, the greater the chances that any problems can be recognized early, before they become serious. Care can be provided according to a thoughtful plan, preventing emotional and financial stress.

In truth, all seniors have special needs. They need help if they are to enjoy their dream retirement and still provide a legacy for their loved ones. For many of the problems that might arise, this book will provide enough information to help you deal with the financial issues of aging, no matter what your present stage of life. Happily ever after does not have to be reserved for fairy tales alone.

978-0-595-39481-4
0-595-39481-7

Printed in the United States
57740LVS00004B/313-471

9 780595 394814